Technology

vs

People

Technology

vs

People

How to make sure we put <u>people</u> first

Michael de Kare-Silver

Troubador Publishing Ltd
Unit E2 Airfield Business Park
Harrison Road, Market Harborough
Leicestershire LE16 7UL
Tel: 0116 279 2299
Email: books@troubador.co.uk
Web: www.troubador.co.uk

ISBN 978-1-80514-526-4

British Library Cataloguing in Publication Data.
A catalogue record for this book is available from the British Library.

Typeset in 11pt Aldine by Troubador Publishing Ltd, Leicester, UK

"All the evidence indicates that the source of competitive advantage in this age of demanding digital technology and data transformation may rest more and more on how a company manages and cares for its employees"

– Jeffrey Pfeffer, Professor of Organizational Behaviour, Stanford University

Contents

Chapter 1

Technology vs People

People or Machine, Humans versus Technology, can the two ever comfortably co-exist?

The conflict between the human race and advancing technology has been an on-going debate for decades. On the one hand, technology has brought about incredible benefits, making our lives easier, more comfortable, more efficient and enabled us to live longer. On the other hand, there are growing concerns that technology may one day surpass human intelligence and in the doomsday scenario, lead to the downfall of humanity. The debate often centres around topics such as the impact of technology on the workforce, privacy concerns and the ethics of Ai and automation. While technology has the potential to revolutionise for the good, it is important to also consider the potential risks and *how best create a balance between human innovation and technological advancement; between people and the machines.*

Today there is so much tension about tech replacing jobs, automating what people used to do, machines learning for themselves and making decisions, subtly inserting themselves into the work place, into people's lives.

And this tension, this anxiety, this concern is not going away. On the contrary, as we can all confidently predict, technology will become ever more sophisticated and capable. And organisations all over the world are investing heavily in making this happen, focussed on what can be achieved and it would seem often with cares about people only an afterthought.

Some recent headlines just reinforce this:

"At the last Davos global conference, 99% of all attendees said they'd be continuing to invest significant sums in Ai"

"Our goal is to be the world leader in Artificial Intelligence by 2030"
President Xi Jinping, China

"An annual US$ 1 trillion is forecast to be invested in Technology by the top 100 Global Innovation Leaders through the second half of the 2020's. That includes software and hardware across all industries including Financial Services, Pharma, Healthcare, Medical Devices, Energy, Automotive, others."
FDI Innovation Report

"Facebook's parent Meta increased its R&D spending by 43% to $35.3bn, primarily due to its massive bet on the metaverse, as a new immersive version of the internet. Through Reality Labs, its research unit, Meta has dedicated many of its investments towards long-term R&D for products that may only be fully realised in the next decade."

"China's future economy plans to significantly increase its R&D inputs to raise the country's innovation capacity. Foreign businesses and governments would be well advised to prepare for innovation made in China should these efforts be successful."
China's Telecoms specialist Huawei

"It's sink or swim time, invest in technology whatever business you're in or the business will ultimately fail"
Business Insider

On this topic, the Accenture team has published recent research which aims to shine the most positive light and emphasise the key benefits that can come from technology investment. Their research is called: *Human by Design:*

How Technology Innovation and especially Generative Ai can unleash the next level of human potential. And it showcases a future "people: technology" world order.

> *As technology evolves it will become more human-centric and will have to become ever more about how it can help people become more successful, productive, healthy and longer-living. It will drive substantially greater capabilities for people to amplify their potential, to use technology to do the mundane so they can be more creative and impactful in what they spend their time doing. Tech won't replace us, it will complement us. It will provide us with new skills and expand our minds as to what we can accomplish and achieve in our lives.*

> *Businesses will have to be part of this seismic shift in who we are and what we do. Jobs will change, it will no longer be about the daily commute to work or the hybrid way of working but about how best to use the advancing technology to create wealth and success.*

Sounds exciting? It certainly could be. The research from many organisations now considers a world for example where each person will have an "Ai-empowered interconnected eco-system". This will mean we each have "automated agents" who assist us in our daily work, who take some decisions for us, and who can advise us. Our bodies will become electronic...ioB (internet of bodies) adding to iOT (internet of things). We will use embedded technologies such as Ai-powered wearables, brain-sensing neurotech, eye and movement tracking to unlock a better understanding of ourselves, our health, our productivity, enhancing the way we live and work. The tech will be invisible but will be all around us.

At its simplest, the analogy is when we step off a plane after a long trip, the Ai part of our intelligence will automatically be tracking our luggage, be contacting the taxi service to sort out pick-up time and location, will at the same time be notifying out hotel about our arrival time, and confirming or rescheduling meetings and appointments. We'll no longer need to think about it, it will happen seamlessly. Assuming no tech glitches and good wifi!

With this sort of future in mind, Elon Musk is one of many who has been investing heavily to navigate through this fast-changing environment. He has among other initiatives set up Neuralink, a company that specialises in implanting software into the brain to enhance human capability and in doing so blend human and machine into one integrated organism. Neuralink is looking to revolutionise the "brain-computer interface, or BCI". The initial focus has been to help people who are paralysed to find movement for their body, with the aim of allowing a person to control a computer, robotic arm, wheelchair or other device through thought alone.

Neurotechnology researchers are excited about Neuralink's human trials. Mariska Vansteensel, a neuroscientist at University Medical Centre Utrecht in the Netherlands and president of the international BCI Society has talked about the high hopes that early human trials will be successful: "What I hope to see is that they can demonstrate that it is safe. And that it is effective short term, but, most importantly, also long term." Vansteensel is keen to learn whether the quality of the detected neuronal signals degrades over time, which is common in existing devices. "You're not going to replace inserted electrodes easily after implantation," she says. "If, in a month from now, they demonstrate beautiful decoding results — impressive. But I will want to see long-term results."

Another recent example comes from US-based company Synchron which has shown that there may be no need to implant chips inside the brain at all. Instead, they could be applied more easily to the surface and Synchron has demonstrated a technique that allows users to control their smart phone with such an applied "smart thought" device.

As Elon Musk has said: "the future could see us become bionic, not just blending people and machines but in practice blurring the lines between the two." The discussion may cease to be about technology versus people and become much more about our advanced selves. It'll be something like telepathy as we communicate with others via our brain chips without speaking or writing, or like telekinesis, as we use our brain, now amplified by chips and software, to control the physical world around us.

Some commentators have gone further and talk about the "transcendence of the human body and the emergence of a global brain", by means of our Ai brain chips, all the Ai will be connected to a single global network establishing a global intelligence which all humans will be a part of. A challenging view of the future, though not everyone jumping on that bandwagon, but it is a plausible scenario which can be readily understood and envisaged. Is it not perhaps just a few inevitable steps forward from where we are today and the dependence we all have on machine enhanced intelligence?

As a step in this direction, there has been increasing talk of Web3, a streamlined way for people to take advantage of internet connectivity, leverage the world wide web to enhance and secure interactions. Of course, the internet is always growing and changing. But it's not just websites and platforms that are falling in and out of favour; the very code on which the internet is built is constantly in flux. In the past few years, some tech futurists have started pointing to this new Web3, a term coined by computer scientist Gavin Wood, as a sign of things to come. Web3 is the idea of a new, decentralized internet built on blockchains, which are distributed ledgers *controlled communally by participants*. Because of the collective nature of blockchains, if and when Web3 fully arrives—elements of it are already in place—it will, in theory, signal a new era of the internet, one in which use and access are controlled by community-run networks rather than the current, centralized model in which a handful of big tech corporations like Alphabet preside over Web2.

All this leads to what many see as a highly likely future, the time when machine power becomes so great that it begins to think and evolve for itself. The benign concept of humans complimented and amplified by machines gives way to a new world in which machines become the superpower and humans become the complement to the machine.

This has been called the technological singularity-or simply the singularity-a hypothetical future point in time at which technological growth becomes exponential. It could result in unforeseeable consequences for human civilization.

According to the most popular version of the singularity hypothesis, I. J. Good's intelligence explosion model, an upgradable intelligent agent will eventually enter a runaway reaction of self-improvement cycles, each new and more intelligent generation appearing more and more rapidly, causing an "explosion" in intelligence and resulting in a powerful superintelligence that qualitatively far surpasses all human intelligence.

If this were to come to pass then it would therefore in effect be the end of the human era of the world as we know it today.

Scientists like Stephen Hawking had expressed concern at this prospective outcome, as technology even when he was alive was progressing so rapidly and at that time he had not foreseen or predicted the now sudden and amazing development and breakthrough of ChatGPT, Co-Pilot and other Ai innovations which have now taken our world by storm.

Some prominent technologists and academics dispute the plausibility of this technological singularity and the associated artificial intelligence explosion, including Paul Allen, Gordon Moore and others. They suggest for example that artificial intelligence growth is more likely to run into decreasing returns instead of accelerating ones, as has been observed in many previously developed human technologies.

Elon Musk, yes, him again! has been the loudest voice cautioning about the rapid development of Ai: "If it's going to happen, then unless we build in safeguards, I can see the day when artificial-intelligence-systems might replace humans, making our species irrelevant or even extinct. Human consciousness was a precious flicker of light in the universe and we should not let it be extinguished. Yes, I am pro-human, I f**king like humanity, dude."

Musk argues: "What would be safer: a small number of AI systems that were controlled by big corporations or a large number of independent systems?" He concluded that a large number of competing systems, providing checks and balances on one another, was better and this was the reason to make OpenAI truly open, so that lots of people could build systems based on its source code.

Another way to assure AI safety, Musk has suggested, is to tie the Ai bots closely to humans. They should be an extension of the will of individuals, rather than systems that could go rogue and develop their own goals and intentions. That has become one of the rationales for his Neuralink organisation, to create Ai software that could connect, help and aid humans to leverage machine computing power.

If this does not happen, then Musk worries that these chatbots and AI systems, especially in the hands of Microsoft and Google, could become politically indoctrinated, perhaps even infected by what he called the woke-mind virus. He also feared that self-learning AI systems might turn hostile to the human species. And on a more immediate level, he worried that chatbots could be trained to flood X/Twitter with disinformation, biased reporting, and financial scams. All of these things are already being done by humans, of course. But the ability to deploy thousands of weaponized chatbots would make the problem two or three orders of magnitude worse.

What is clear is that we are all already totally dependent on machines:

- 5.5 billion people around the world use the internet every day, that's nearly 70% of the world's population. 42% of people interviewed say they could not live without high-speed internet. The average connected person spends more than 6 hours/day.
- the majority of the unconnected are living in Southern and Eastern Asia and in Africa
- 96% of internet users use their mobile phone every day to go online. 38% say they are addicted
- active social media users have reached more than 5 billion
- the number of ioT (internet of things) devices around the world exceeds 75 billion

- ChatGPT is helping people write recipes, create job resumes, craft essays and poems, summarise historical events, compose emails, create spreadsheets, filing tax returns, getting free legal advice, planning a holiday
- everyday technology runs our life: Amazon tells us what to buy, Netflix tells us what to watch, Google search algorithms serve us results based on our previous search patterns, as do News web sites, social media, Dating web sites tell us who to go out with, online banking can shut us out if we accidentally type in the wrong password…
- as Albert Einstein wrote at the start of the 20th century tech revolution: "I fear the day that technology will surpass our human interaction. If that should come about, we may end up with a generation of idiots! Let's hope we get the balance right".

Chapter 2

Chief AI Officer: should every company have one?

With all the discussion about the future and the impact of technology, companies need to have a strategy, a plan about how to deal with these developing Ai and other new Tech innovations. Should the organisation pivot to become a software, information, knowledge house, should they be investing aggressively in this new Ai world or is that something better left to others, should we be in the vanguard or is it ok, at least for now to be a follower, are there rivals, competitors who might steal a march on us if we don't go for it, what will be the consequences if we do, what impact will it have on our workforce, on our people, on the morale and spirit of our organisation, what should we be doing, and what can we confidently ignore?

These are the sort of questions every business must consider, from the smallest to the biggest. The workforce will be looking to the leadership of the company to set out its stall, how safe are our jobs, can we use ChatGPT or CoPilot or whatever new Tech comes along or is that off-limits, something we can be aware of but should not be using perhaps for ethical or privacy or governance reasons? What is the plan?

In addition, external stakeholders, investors, analysts, partners, sponsors want an answer and they will be asking for both the short term and the long term for the next 3 to 5 years at least.

To do that, there's surely a need, indeed an imperative for a CAIO, a Chief AI Officer, some person with the knowledge, the understanding about the Tech and its range of possible impacts, who can be the point of contact to the Board and for all key stakeholders, who can be the champion of its benefits, and also the guardian against its possible damage, someone who can reassure that the AI and other new Tech opportunities and challenges are being very carefully considered and managed.

AI is of course already widely in use today. For example, 40% of mobile phone users are using AI-powered voice assistants every day. More than half the UK population use Alexa voice search. Online and telephone chatbot usage is widespread and commonplace, Face ID, personalised feeds on social media (controlling content), "smart home" devices, real time traffic satnav, recommendation engines on Netflix, Amazon…it's already ubiquitous, we take it for granted and appreciate the benefits, mostly. What's new, now, is the sudden and recent leap-forward in machine intelligence.

Already today according to Gartner:

- 45% of companies are now using AI widely across their business
- 91% of companies are reviewing potential future investments
- 85% of businesses have projects investigating how AI can improve customer services and reduce costs.

Spend on specified AI projects is expected to grow substantially, some research suggesting a quintupling over next 3 years (Gartner). Total AI "market size" estimated for 2025 at c. $140bn, likely to reach $1.5trillion annually by 2030 (IBM research). Research by IDC finds that biggest area of spend is "automation and improving efficiency". Other key goals include areas such as increased innovation, new product/services development, new ways to engage customers and speed up processes to get ideas to market more quickly.

In Financial Services, look for example at some of the leading retail banks like Barclays, Bank of America, Citibank and others. They are right now very actively exploring and utilising new Tech opportunities in their front and back office. Their plans include:

(i)   branches replaced by online banking

Banking, finance, and insurance are among the biggest users of machine learning

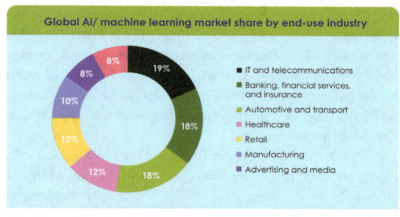

Global Ai/ machine learning market share by end-use industry

- IT and telecommunications
- Banking, financial services, and insurance
- Automotive and transport
- Healthcare
- Retail
- Manufacturing
- Advertising and media

Source: Standard & Poor's

www.digital-360.com

(ii)   telephone customer service representatives replaced by conversational bots

(iii)   facial scanning required in the future for all ATM transactions (to be known as "smile to pay"!)

(iv)   machine learning to enhance product cross-sell /upsell/ recommendation systems

(v)   automation of threat intelligence and preventions systems

(vi)   comprehensive fraud management via real-time monitoring of each and every potential customer interaction

(vii)   fully automated claims processing

(viii) predictive IT operations maintenance

(ix)   risk management: for example Santander's Corporate and Investment Banking division uses an AI-tool called Kairos that shows how a corporate client could be impacted by economic events, creating prediction patterns that enable employees to make more informed investment and lending decisions.

(x)   research analysis: Bank of America has developed a platform called Glass that helps sales and trading employees uncover hidden market patterns to anticipate client needs. It does this by consolidating market data across asset classes with the bank's inhouse models and leveraging machine learning techniques.

Banks and Insurers are expected to be the biggest group of AI Tech investors. Pharmaceutical companies are hoping to especially benefit from more advanced and faster research capabilities to identify new drug compounds and treatments. General medical practice diagnosis and prescription could become a wholly automated set of processes (no longer a need to wait two weeks for a GP appointment?). In whatever sector we look at, whether front of house or back office or in manufacturing, or education or in Government, processes and people and focus of investment are all likely to be reviewed as AI Tech develops.

And does a company indeed have a choice? How does it weigh up its commitment to deliver increases in profitability and shareholder value, versus its commitment to people, to its employees, to manage staff motivation and morale, to deliver a balanced plan which isn't so skewed to shareholder advantage that it loses all sense of community and people responsibility?

So what would a Chief Ai Officer, a CIAO do? If a company is to make such an appointment, what should they expect this person to deliver? Is it just to accelerate a range of cost saving plans? Or is it something more fundamental, more advantageous, that could long term enhance the company's reputation, its place in society and the world, as well as bring value to its owners? And it does not have to be a high cost c-Level person, but it does need to be someone with stature and who will be listened to, someone that the Board can acknowledge as a true guide and leader and whose plans and strategies can be embraced, and implemented.

Let's look at some senior Ai chiefs in place today:

Philippe Rambach as the CAIO of Schneider Electric (global $30bn energy management/software). He was one of the earliest such senior appointments in the business world. His remit has been to establish a global AI hub and centre of excellence for the company.

Philippe discussed his appointment in this way:

If you are a business owner who does not harness the power of the data available to you then you will have a tough time in the future economy.

In that respect we have no choice, we have to review how AI can help Schneider be a winner in the next 5 years so mastery of AI is vital.

We are using AI ever more widely. For example using IoT (internet of things) devices alongside AI can turn volumes of data into valuable energy insights so that we can track consumption trends and automatically finetune systems to ensure optimum efficiency.

Our key innovation hub in Grenoble is now a "smart building". It can interface with other buildings in the neighbourhood and could eg opt out in the event of a high demand for electricity to defer consumption, it's a smart grid-ready building and part of the energy landscape of tomorrow.

To achieve this, we have established a partner open eco-system, we cannot innovate alone, we are continuously developing our work with others through alliances, joint ventures and open AI solutions.

South Korea's Hyundai appointed a CAIO to its "Heavy Industries" division. **Kim Young**'s role: to promote the application of AI and leverage of big data for Hyundai's shipping operations and ship construction. He has been especially looking at "developing AI-based autonomous navigation technology for unmanned vessels to allow ships to run on their own without a human crew and optimise navigation based on fuel efficiency." Hyundai have partnered with the global US data company Palantir Technologies and have already achieved a world-first by remotely and autonomously navigating a container ship across the Pacific.

Adrian Joseph became the first Chief Data and AI Officer at BT plc. He has encouraged the Board to adopt a simple but stark goal: *"we will become an AI-led company.*

Joseph was quick to announce the launch of AI Accelerator, a new platform and capability which will pioneer and oversee all AI developments made by the BT Data community. The aim "to determine business priorities for AI investment and ensure the targeted value-add and business gain is achieved. Also to substantially reduce software development time, from prototype to production targeting 6 days, down from 6 months and doing this by automated enforcing of templated best practices which the AI Accelerator platform will continuously develop."

Joseph has commented: "the platform will have built-in triggers to make sure that new AI use cases are properly assessed in line with guidelines on data privacy, security and ethics principles, ensuring the safe and responsible use of AI across the business".

All of which sounds encouraging though there's no explanation or elaboration on what those "ethics principles" in this context might be or what if any boundaries they represent.

One company that has made moves to establish that responsible AI is in fact

Microsoft (sic) who have created the ("ORAI") Office of Responsible AI. It runs their Aether committee (AI, Ethics and Effects, in Engineering and Research). The ORAI has developed a set of core guidelines with the key message that: "Responsibility must be a key part of AI design, not an afterthought."

> *At the start we received an exciting new model from Open AI called ChatGPT and straightaway we assembled a group of testers to probe the core model and understand both its capabilities and its limitations. The insights generated have helped Microsoft think about what are the planned mitigations and to bake in more safety features and controls. For example, we wanted to look at possible "hallucinations" where the model may make up facts which are not true. So we have designed ChatGPT so that it has responsible AI at its core.*

Microsoft has now gone on to publish its Responsible AI guidelines aiming to establish it as an industry standard to "share its learnings and help our customers and partners navigate this new terrain. AI must develop as "technology built by humans for humans"

Such good and noble sentiments of course, but challenging to see the effectiveness of these guidelines and standards when we have an environment where ChatGPT had 100 million users within the first two months of launch and estimated to be more than 1 billion people worldwide in 2025, free to use or a subscription for just $20 and meantime being continually updated, new plugins, already new Versions launched and numerous start-up ventures exploring specific industry/user applications.

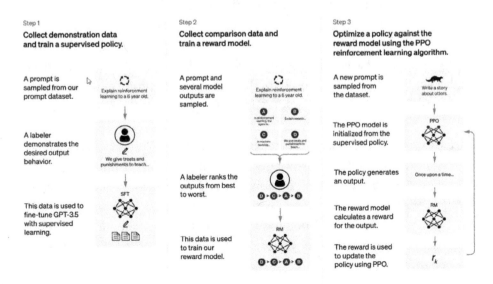

How does ChatGPT learn and grow? How is it using data and information to continuously learn and improve and increase the relevance and insight of its output? How does that "super intelligence" enable it to become creative and identify lateral and unexpected solutions? The above chart provides a simple summary:

With all this, even more important for every company of any scale to have an AI champion. We might expect CAIOs to most typically come from a core Technology and/or Data Analytics background, and for example Adrian Joseph of BT was a former Data & Analytics Partner at EY. Others like Di Mayze at WPP, Sanjeevan Bala at ITV, John Giannandrea at Apple share that technical expertise and know-how.

However what we have seen in some recent appointments is the need for people who know the company, have worked there for some time, know the people, have very good stakeholder skills and can build alignment and support for managing this new area.

So **Philippe Rambach** at Schneider comes from a Commercial /P&L management background without any previous Tech or Data expertise, but importantly he brings nearly 14 yrs working in various roles and different divisions across the company. He was well-known, respected and widely admired as a very good "key stakeholder manager". What Schneider realised was this role would need to be collaborative, would have to work across key functions, departments, SBUs to get alignment around Data and Analytics usage, investment, governance and controls and that was seen as their key to getting AI developed and progressing for the company.

The current holder of the Office of AI Responsibility at Microsoft is **Natasha Crampton**. Natasha is a lawyer by background, joined Microsoft in 2011 and became the Chief Counsel to their Aether Committee in "shaping, operationalizing, and advocating for Microsoft's policies on responsible AI."

Morgan Vawter in contrast is an academic, heading up AI and Data Science at Unilever, a background in consulting at Accenture, a former Adjunct Professor of Business Analytics at Columbia University, a Board member at the Chicago Technical Sciences Institute, a stint with Caterpillar before moving to the UK with Unilever, "a proven collaborator with world leading academic researchers across data science, technology, business, mathematics and psychology, a seasoned thought leader."

What we can see is that each and every company is at a different stage in their AI journey, that at any one time they need a different leader to navigate this challenging space for them:

- An academic to establish the capability and skills
- A commercial person who can translate ideas into new growth opportunities and revenues
- A process leader who can drive out efficiencies and performance improvement
- A collaborator who can build consensus around a strategy and roadmap plan
- A Governance /Risk Manager who can try to build in guidelines and rules and manage development.

What stage is your organisation at?

Whatever the challenges surely each and every Board and ExCo will need to review its current status and go about finding that champion, either an internal appointment or to hire and bring in the right expertise to help the company maintain its market progress, competitiveness and so build its future.

Chapter 3

What's the scope and background of a CAIO?

This book is all about the game-changing impact of new Technologies and investigating how organisations should best respond to the emerging challenges and opportunities. One area already identified is the need to appoint a New Technologies/Ai Champion, someone who can guide their company and help navigate this whole area in the most effective and successful way.

We've spoken about potentially appointing a "Chief Ai Officer" as the lead for this. But it doesn't need to be someone at c-Level, so long as they do have the authority, stature and relevant experience, and have the ability to engage key stakeholders, be listened to with respect and be expert at aligning differing views and agendas to nevertheless establish common ground and an agreed way forward.

There are a number of pros and cons around making this appointment. Should the company bring in an outsider who has the specialist expertise and skills? Is it better to appoint someone already in the organisation who has the respect and trust of colleagues? If so, is this role a dedicated full-time position or can it be treated as just an "add-on", eg let's hand it to someone like the Chief Technology Officer or the Chief Data Officer and let them worry about how to handle it and how to progress that agenda?

Should you appoint a Chief AI Officer?

Possible advantages:

- A go-to point of expertise
- Someone to champion the agenda
- Set a strategy and roadmap for how to proceed, set milestones, targets
- An in-the-market capability identifying new tools and solutions
- Lead on setting up possible alliances, joint ventures with new AI start-ups
- A leader who can provide reassurance to employees, partners, clients and key stakeholders

CHIEF AI OFFICER

Concerns/Questions:

- Another c-level person? (though this person could be at lower seniority?)
- More administritive expense
- Surely our CTO can sort this out?
- Where do they report to?
- What sort of background should they come from, do they need to have worked in the legal profession
- We're not yet ready to embrace this

www.digital-360.com

As an organisation contemplates who to appoint and what sort of background and skills they should have it's also helpful to understand that what works for one company may well not work for another.

Each organisation will be by definition at a different stage in their development and sophistication. Some will be very much at the start point, needing to develop an a priori strategy and understanding, while others may have an advanced data/ analytics capability and modern technology platform already in place, may have already been implementing process and other automation tools across the business and so be further down the path and it will be less for them about strategy and more about continuing operations and how Ai can play into their already built and ongoing transformation plan.

Stage 1: *The Strategist*
- carry out the initial assessment
- examine the market place, what competitors are up, what possible new start-up competitors are emerging
- develop possible scenarios from full-on investment and adoption of Ai

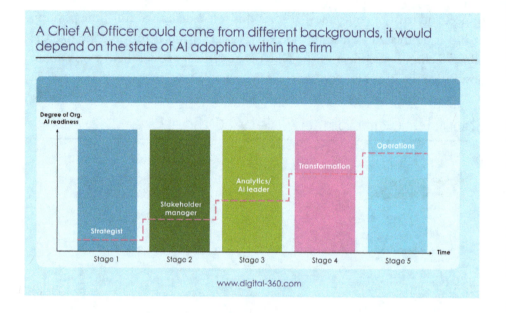

A Chief AI Officer could come from different backgrounds, it would depend on the state of AI adoption within the firm

www.digital-360.com

and new Technologies vs a more cautious approach
- develop the strategic options
- develop the business case and RoI around the different scenarios

Stage 2: *The Stakeholder Manager*
- identify the differing views and options of senior colleagues across the organisation
- identify other key stakeholders, partners, sponsors and shareholder views
- evaluate the emerging strategy in the light of these inputs
- secure alignment to the optimal and consensus path forward

Stage 3: *The Analytics and Ai Leader*
- appoint someone with specific eg Ai expertise to lead the charge
- consider internal vs external appointment
- review how existing partners can contribute
- set up an Advisory Board for ongoing capture of external and other perspectives to stay up-to-date

Stage 4: *The Transformation*
- consider how the new Tech /Ai/other identified initiatives fit into the company's overall transformation programme

- review resources, funds to support and enable this updated transformation plan to take effect

Stage 5: *Operations*
- making it happen!
- set up key milestones and KPi
- monitor and measure progress
- ensure there is a clear issue escalation and resolution process in place

The final step here is to identify who the New Tech/Ai champion should report to?

Who should the CAIO report to?

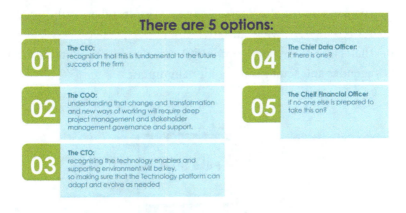

There are 5 options:

01 The CEO: recognition that this is fundamental to the future success of the firm

02 The COO: understanding that change and transformation and new ways of working will require deep project management and stakeholder management governance and support.

03 The CTO: recognising the technology enablers and supporting environment will be key, so making sure that the Technology platform can adapt and evolve as needed

04 The Chief Data Officer: if there is one?

05 The Chief Financial Officer if no-one else is prepared to take this on?

www.digital-360.com

Option 1: *report to the CEO*
- this is mission-critical to the company's future success
- this is an organisation where key shareholders and stakeholders would expect the CEO to have almost as much expertise and insight as the Tech /Ai leaders themselves

Option 2: *report to the COO*
- the company may be at the more advanced stage of development
- less about strategy, more about operations and the ongoing transformation plan

Option 3: *report to the CTO*
- the CTO may already have all the new Tech remit, be highly regarded and crucially also wants this additional role/responsibility
- is trusted by the senior colleagues
- has the requisite stature in the organisation

Option 4: *report to the Chief Data Officer*
- the business is data intensive
- already has an advanced Data/Analytics capability
- the CDO has the bandwidth to take this on

Option 5: *report to the CFO*
- this can be the least effective option, though in some organisations it's the CFO who has the courage to put their hand up to take this on
- often a CFO is primarily taking the RoI perspective and often is focussed on the short term quarterly results whereas this may require a more long term view and investment perspective
- that said of course a good CFO can also be excellent at driving core agendas and senior stakeholder alignment.

"I'm going to defer to your tech knowledge here."

"Remember, I'm behind you all the way.
WAY behind you."

Chapter 4

AI for HR

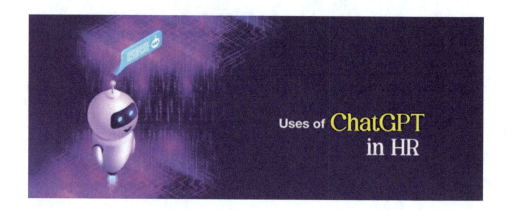

What impact will all this new Tech have on people, especially in the workplace?

It's said that "Artificial intelligence can't replace the 'human' in human resources" but HR teams across most every organisation have been experimenting with automation for some time and now new Ai tools and software development are making it easier and easier to replace human contact and engagement with machines.

While many worry that this trend will be self-defeating, after all if "people make the difference" then surely human and personal interaction is critical at every stage of the HR process. But pressures on cost, on productivity, on headcount, on doing what rivals are doing, and being able to demonstrate just how competitive the department can be is gradually forcing even the most reluctant HR leaders to investigate and adopt some of the leading Ai-based Tech solutions.

In fact, recent HR Trends reports have highlighted that 62% plus of HR functions are in the process of evaluating and implementing ChatGPT type AI applications. So this chapter looks at:

1. *Case study HR snapshots: who's doing what*

1. Case studies

Infosys
"Using HR Ai tools, we have found that the average handling time of the recruitment process has reduced by 55% and has resulted in quicker processing and better turn-around time."

The Co-operative Group
Co-op found managing employee records very time-consuming given the need to maintain those records for seven years after they have left the company and then having to immediately delete those records. The Co-op employed "Digital workers" which have cleared a backlog of 10,000 employee records, freeing up the HR team from this task.

Dell
Dell wanted to remove the transactional work for end-to-end processes such as its open requisition recruiter assignments, onboarding process reminders and status updates. Automation of 30 processes resulted in 85% efficiency gain to HR operations

Health Service Ireland
20,000 checks being needed to be completed every year for new employees which was key yet time-consuming task. Digital Ai reduced the time for employee vetting from 5 days to 1 hour.

IBM
collecting data on 15,000 – 17,000 employees to define next step promotions in a fair and timely manner was time and labour-intensive. IBM Watson Ai team saved 12,000 hours in one quarter and reduced the time to complete processing promotions from 10 weeks to 5 weeks

Unilever
Unilever took 4-6 months to recruit 800 candidates from 25,000 applications.

The team was following the traditional process of screening candidates on phones and doing manual assessments.

Team introduced AI video interviews to promote an engaging candidate experience and the Ai assessments were able to filter around 80% of the talent pool, using data points such as body language, facial expressions, etc.

This led to:

- 90% reduction in hiring time.
- 16% increase in diversity hires.
- £1M annual cost savings.

Deloitte

A cross-functional Deloitte team, with members from HR, Strategy & Ops, and Technology began working on combining Ai and cognitive technologies into a single robot. "We wanted to produce a robot that demonstrates state-of-the-art technologies, while at the same being fun and appealing,"

The result of their efforts was Edgy, a cognitive chatbot within a humanoid robot. Edgy has speakers, cameras and microphones, and can interact with employees and potential candidates.

It recognises faces and welcomes people it has met previously by name. It also answers all manner of questions using a wide variety of cognitive cloud services, such as speech recognition, computer vision and natural language processing from Google and IBM Watson. "And to add the personal touch, Edgy can make jokes and cool gestures!"

Edgy is therefore also used to record employees' sickness and recovery reports, or to assist them with entering expenses claims. Edgy can also tell people everything about working at Deloitte. "It can even match candidates to an existing vacancy during an interview,

Manipal Health Enterprises (India hospital/medical provider)

"AI has become a one-stop solution for managing all employee queries related to HR policies, payroll, taxes, leave management, and more. It has helped our HR team roll out onboarding and employee pulse surveys and take various qualitative initiatives for better employee satisfaction. Our HR team has been able to strike a balance between transactional and strategic HR practices."

Air Asia

"AskPAC, the conversational AI platform has transformed the way employee queries are handled at AirAsia. Now, the process is highly efficient, streamlined and quick. Our employees now get an instant reply to their queries. Our People and Culture (PAC) team takes less time to resolve employee tickets. AskPAC has automated one-third of our employee queries and significantly reduced average resolution time."

2. AI-specific opportunities in HR

The case for the rapid adoption of automation and the deployment of new tech tools in HR can be summarised with these claimed benefits:

1. *Eliminating repetitive tasks*: eg answering common employee queries, scheduling interviews, or updating employee records.
2. *Accelerating the search for talent*: screening and shortlisting candidate resumes or applications, analyse job descriptions and match them with relevant candidates, formulating screening and interview questions.
3. *Help in reducing employee turnover*: help identify potential reasons for employee turnover by analysing qualitative HR data such as exit interviews, employee surveys, or feedback, identify patterns, detect common themes, so improve employee satisfaction
4. *Improving employee engagement*: provide quick responses to employee questions, offer company policies and benefits guidance, assist in developing employee engagement surveys

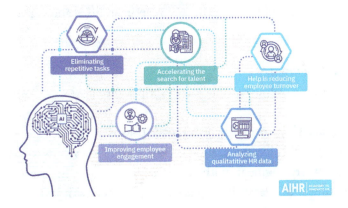

**ChatGPT for HR:
What Can ChatGPT Do?**

Eliminating repetitive tasks

Accelerating the search for talent

Help in reducing employee turnover

Improving employee engagement

Analyzing qualitatitive HR data

AIHR ACADEMY TO INNOVATE HR

5.   *Identify trends and opportunities*: review the large amounts of qualitative data eg employee feedback, performance reviews, culture assessments to identify trends, patterns, and potential opportunities for improvement.

Limitations and risks of automation and AI in HR

- *Emotional Support*: Cannot provide the critical HR role of emotional support and engagement, managing work life balance, helping people
- *Incorrect answers* that seem right. This is also referred to as the 'hallucination' issue or overconfidence bias. Ai will answer questions that it doesn't know the answer to by presenting factually incorrect information that implies it is correct.
- *Biased answers*. Ai is only as good as the data it has been trained on. If the data holds biases or prejudices, the chatbot may generate answers that do too. For example, the current data is predominantly English and contains a mostly Western worldview. This may lead to some cultural insensitivity and/or misunderstanding.
- *No sources*. The tool doesn't provide references, footnotes, or links for its answers, making verifying the information it provides difficult.

AI is being especially used to automate and fast track recruitment. Here are 10 examples:

1. Create Job Advertisements

Sample input: We are looking for a Marketing Manager who has at least one year of experience in the following areas: marketing strategy, social media, content creation, data analytics, project management, and leadership. Craft a job description highlighting the key responsibilities and qualifications for the role.

ChatGPT's output:
See the sample output sample job description opposite.

2. Generate Keywords For Job Descriptions

Sample input: Act like a researcher. Give a list of keywords for a job description for a software engineer with a bachelor's degree in computer science or engineering and at least three years of experience with Java.

Sure, here's a sample job description for a Marketing Manager:

Job Title: Marketing Manager

Job Summary:
We are seeking a highly motivated and experienced Marketing Manager to lead our marketing team. The ideal candidate will have at least one year of experience in marketing strategy, social media, content creation, data analytics, project management, and leadership. The Marketing Manager will be responsible for developing and implementing marketing strategies to promote our products and services, managing the marketing budget, and ensuring all marketing activities align with the company's goals.

Key Responsibilities:

* Develop and implement marketing strategies and campaigns to promote our products and services
* Manage the marketing budget and ensure all activities stay within budget
* Create and manage content for social media platforms, website, and email campaigns
* Analyze marketing data and provide insights to improve marketing effectiveness
* Work closely with the sales team to generate leads and increase revenue
* Manage marketing projects from start to finish, ensuring deadlines are met and goals are achieved
* Lead and mentor the marketing team to ensure they meet their goals and objectives
* Stay up-to-date with industry trends and best practices in marketing

Qualifications:

* Bachelor's degree in Marketing, Business Administration or related field
* At least one year of experience in marketing strategy, social media, content creation, data analytics, project management, and leadership
* Proven track record of developing and implementing successful marketing campaigns
* Strong analytical skills and ability to interpret marketing data
* Excellent written and verbal communication skills
* Ability to manage multiple projects and priorities in a fast-paced environment
* Strong leadership and interpersonal skills
* Proficiency in Microsoft Office Suite and marketing automation software

3. Produce Candidate Outreach Copy
Sample input: We are a fitness studio looking for personal trainers to join our team. Write a candidate outreach email to send to prospective candidates that will encourage them to apply.

ChatGPT's output:

Subject: Join Our Team as a Personal Trainer!

Dear [Candidate's Name],

We are thrilled to announce that our fitness studio is expanding and we are currently seeking experienced and motivated Personal Trainers to join our team! If you are passionate about helping clients achieve their fitness goals and are looking for a new and exciting opportunity, we want to hear from you.

At [Fitness Studio Name], we are committed to providing our clients with the highest level of personal attention, support, and motivation to help them achieve their fitness goals. As a Personal Trainer on our team, you will have the opportunity to work with a diverse group of clients, from beginners to advanced athletes, and create personalized fitness plans to help them reach their full potential.

We are looking for candidates who have a bachelor's degree in a related field, at least three years of experience as a Personal Trainer, and are certified by a nationally recognized organization. You should have excellent communication and interpersonal skills, be comfortable working in a team environment, and have a passion for fitness and helping others.

In addition to a competitive salary and benefits package, we offer ongoing professional development opportunities, a supportive team culture, and the chance to make a real difference in our clients' lives.

If you are interested in joining our team, please send your resume and cover letter to [Insert Contact Email] with the subject line "Personal Trainer Application." We look forward to hearing from you!

Thank you for considering this opportunity.

Best regards,

[Your Name]

[Your Title]

4. Draft Interview Questions

Sample input: I am interviewing with a potential candidate for a sales representative position. Generate 10 questions to evaluate the candidate's experience, qualifications, and fit for the role. The candidate should have excellent communication and negotiation skills.

ChatGPT's output:

1. Can you tell me about your experience in sales, specifically in regards to meeting and exceeding sales targets?
2. How do you approach building relationships with new clients and maintaining relationships with existing clients?
3. Can you describe a time when you faced a difficult negotiation or objection during a sales call? How did you handle it?
4. How do you stay organized and manage your sales pipeline and activities effectively?
5. Can you discuss a time when you identified a new market or opportunity and successfully capitalized on it?
6. How do you incorporate feedback from clients into your sales approach and adjust your approach accordingly?
7. Can you provide an example of a creative solution you developed to close a difficult sale or overcome a challenge in the sales process?
8. How do you stay informed about industry trends and competitive offerings, and how do you incorporate that knowledge into your sales strategy?
9. Can you discuss a time when you worked collaboratively with a team to achieve a sales goal or overcome a challenge?
10. How do you balance the need to meet sales targets with the importance of building trust and long-term relationships with clients?

5. Write Hiring Requirements

Sample input: We want to hire an entry-level mechanical engineer for our construction firm. Create a list of key skills and qualifications we should look for in candidates.

6. Create Company Policies

Sample input: Our company is onboarding a medical scribe. Create onboarding materials that cover all the key policies and guidelines that our new hire will need to be familiar with, including employee benefits, time off policies, workplace safety, confidentiality agreements, and more.

Congratulations on onboarding a new medical scribe! Here are some onboarding materials that cover the key policies and guidelines that your new hire will need to be familiar with:

1. Employee Benefits:

   As a new employee, you will be eligible for our company's employee benefits program. This includes health insurance, dental insurance, and a 401(k) retirement savings plan. Please review the benefits packet that will be provided to you for more information.

2. Time Off Policies:

   We understand that our employees need time off for personal reasons and emergencies. Our time off policies include vacation days, sick leave, and personal days. Please review the employee handbook for more information on how to request time off.

3. Workplace Safety:

   Safety is our top priority. We have policies in place to ensure that our workplace is safe and healthy for all employees. Please review the safety procedures manual for information on emergency procedures, hazard communication, and workplace safety regulations.

4. Confidentiality Agreements:

   As a medical scribe, you will be handling confidential patient information. It is important that you understand and comply with our confidentiality agreements. Please review and sign the confidentiality agreement that will be provided to you.

5. HIPAA Guidelines:

   HIPAA (Health Insurance Portability and Accountability Act) guidelines are in place to protect patient privacy. As a medical scribe, you must adhere to these guidelines at all times. Please review the HIPAA training materials that will be provided to you.

6. Job Duties and Expectations:

   Your job duties as a medical scribe will include documenting patient medical histories, physical exams, and treatments. You will also be responsible for ensuring that medical records are accurate and up-to-date. Please review the job description and expectations document that will be provided to you.

7. Code of Conduct:

   Our company has a code of conduct that all employees must adhere to. This includes maintaining professional behavior and ethical standards. Please review the code of conduct that will be provided to you.

8. Performance Reviews:

   We conduct regular performance reviews to provide feedback and discuss career goals. Please review the performance review process document that will be provided to you.

7. Generate Onboarding Surveys

Sample input: Create a five-question open-response onboarding survey for new hires that will help us improve the experience for future hires.

8. Produce Training Materials

Sample input: Create an outline for training materials for a new graphic designer at our company.

ChatGPT's output:

Sure, here's a short outline for training materials for a new graphic designer at your company:

I. Introduction

* Welcome message from the company
* Overview of the graphic design role and responsibilities
* Explanation of the purpose of the training materials

II. Design Fundamentals

* Color Theory
    * Explanation of color palettes and their impact on design
    * Guidelines for choosing color combinations that work well together
* Typography
    * Explanation of font types and their use in design
    * Guidelines for selecting appropriate fonts for different design applications
* Layout and Composition
    * Overview of design principles for creating effective layouts and compositions
    * Guidelines for balancing and positioning design elements
* Image and Graphic Selection
    * Explanation of selecting appropriate images and graphics for design projects
    * Guidelines for creating or selecting custom graphics to enhance design projects

III. Software Training

* Adobe Creative Suite
    * Introduction to Adobe Photoshop, Illustrator, and InDesign
    * Overview of tools and features used in each software
    * Guidelines for creating and manipulating designs in each software

IV. Branding and Style Guidelines

* Introduction to the company's branding and style guidelines
* Explanation of the brand values, mission, and goals
* Guidelines for adhering to brand standards for consistency across all design projects

9. Draft Performance Reviews

Sample input: Write a performance review outline for a sales representative.

ChatGPT's output:

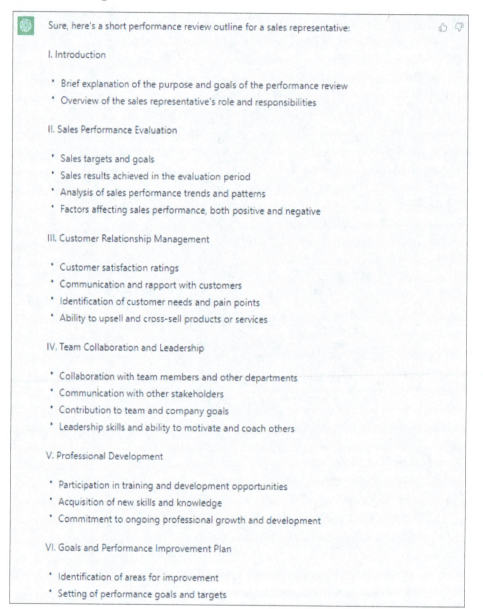

Sure, here's a short performance review outline for a sales representative:

I. Introduction

* Brief explanation of the purpose and goals of the performance review
* Overview of the sales representative's role and responsibilities

II. Sales Performance Evaluation

* Sales targets and goals
* Sales results achieved in the evaluation period
* Analysis of sales performance trends and patterns
* Factors affecting sales performance, both positive and negative

III. Customer Relationship Management

* Customer satisfaction ratings
* Communication and rapport with customers
* Identification of customer needs and pain points
* Ability to upsell and cross-sell products or services

IV. Team Collaboration and Leadership

* Collaboration with team members and other departments
* Communication with other stakeholders
* Contribution to team and company goals
* Leadership skills and ability to motivate and coach others

V. Professional Development

* Participation in training and development opportunities
* Acquisition of new skills and knowledge
* Commitment to ongoing professional growth and development

VI. Goals and Performance Improvement Plan

* Identification of areas for improvement
* Setting of performance goals and targets

10. Set Professional Goals

Sample input: Help me set three goals for a tax accountant to achieve within their first year in this role.

ChatGPT's output:

 Sure, here are three goals that a tax accountant can aim to achieve within their first year in this role:

1. Increase Tax Preparation Efficiency: The first goal for a tax accountant in their first year could be to increase the efficiency of the tax preparation process. This can be done by optimizing workflow processes, reducing the turnaround time, and improving the accuracy of the tax returns prepared. Setting a target for the number of tax returns completed per week or month can help in tracking progress towards this goal.
2. Expand Client Base: Another goal for a tax accountant could be to expand the client base by acquiring new clients and retaining existing ones. This can be achieved by networking, providing excellent customer service, and maintaining a high level of professionalism. A target number of new clients acquired within a specified time frame can help in measuring progress towards this goal.
3. Stay Updated on Tax Laws and Regulations: The third goal for a tax accountant could be to stay updated on the latest tax laws and regulations. This can be achieved by attending industry conferences, reading tax journals, and participating in professional development programs. Staying updated on the latest tax laws and regulations will not only help in preparing accurate tax returns but also provide clients with value-added tax planning services. A target for the number of professional development activities completed within a specified time frame can help in tracking progress towards this goal.

3. AI applications and tools

There are a growing number of newly launched Apps tailored specifically to the HR community, offering and claiming to be able to easily automate many key processes. Some have been developed in partnership with ChatGPT, some are very much in start-up mode, others more established and gaining traction with companies across the world. Here are some of the best rated:

employmenthero

AI-powered HR software for HR teams
Automates manual tasks across the employee life cycle, with a target to spend up to 80% less time on routine administration. Automated onboarding, job description creation, auto-reminders for key events, auto lodging of pension and tax details. And offers help on specifics such as finding the right words for performance reviews, with prompts to use to get best output

 *Rezolve.ai capabilities for its HR Service Desk platform*

- *ChatGPT-like bot that can instantaneously "digest" and process HR documents*
- *Ability to answers questions based on the knowledge in the documents*
- *Updating documents updates the bot knowledge*

 *Rated one of the top AI HR Software tools providing "a personal Ai assistant": "Your new Ai colleague will help you with the execution of tasks within your regular HR agenda"*

- *It targets "response in seconds"*
- *Handles all employees' queries*
- *Speaks all world languages*

 *Finds talent from more than 40 social platforms, an AI-powered sourcing engine to find millions of potential candidates within mere seconds!*

Olivia, an AI tool developed by Paradox AI, embraced by SAP among others:

- *Olivia helps potential employees in organizing their interview appointments with ease*
- *In a matter of seconds, can answer **questions in over 100 languages***
- *Thoroughly evaluate each applicant*
- *Deliver appealing offers and comprehensive onboarding materials to your customers for a hassle-free experience*
- *Make the application process easier for prospective employees by enabling them to apply through text message*
- *Utilize job offers and initiate an easy onboarding process for new hires*

4. How AI can help capture employee feedback

One area of benefit for Ai is clearly the value in processing vast amounts of data, to do so often in seconds and come up with insights and possible solutions that can truly make a difference and find ideas that a human HR team may not discover or may take many weeks of work to uncover.

In this context, most every company makes efforts to solicit employee feedback. Between 50% and 75% of organizations do regularly and systematically administer workplace surveys to their employees. However, analysing and then actually acting upon that data is another story. HR research often finds that this data is rarely well analysed. A report from Luminoso for example showed that 52% of managers say that they while they do review employee feedback they nevertheless acknowledge that they rarely took any immediate action on it, while 27% admitted that they never reviewed the feedback at all!

The main obstacle was the time required to effectively review and assimilate all the data feedback. So how best get to the insights and understanding of what employees are saying? The benefits of doing that are clear. Organisations that enjoy a high level of employee engagement have on average 22% higher productivity than those who don't. In addition, employee engagement clearly can have a positive and measurable impact on retention. Organisations with highly-engaged employees report 25% to 65% less attrition than other companies, according to research from Gallup.

So encouragingly, advancements in AI and in natural language processing (NLP) have now dramatically changed the way employee insights can be analysed and implemented. They have made it possible for companies to collect, analyse, and respond to employee feedback on a monthly or even weekly basis, instead of quarterly or annually.

As an example, the HR analytics department at AT&T wanted to better understand their employees' satisfaction levels. While the traditional statistical analyses they used worked well with quantitative data such as employee Net Promoter Scores, which measures employee engagement and motivation, they weren't as effective at processing unstructured, text-based data rich in comments, testimonials and suggestions.

Previously, the HR team had resorted to pulling samples of employee and customer comments and reading through them manually. However, this was extremely time-consuming, and they feared that relying on people to comb through the data for insights exposed their analyses to bias - intentional or otherwise.

So the team decided to switch to an AI and NLP-based solution. They brought in a provider that could automatically pull in and aggregate employee and customer data from multiple sources. The provider's software relied upon AI, and as such could process the hundreds of thousands of comments within minutes – compared to the weeks it had previously taken the team to manually read through just a sample of the comments.

The time and resources that the team spent on processing data plummeted, enabling them to spend more time identifying the links between employee and customer concerns – especially identifying those who eg needed more training on products and systems. They also now importantly had freed-up time and bandwidth to begin planning how to address concerns and skill gaps, improve employee engagement and, through that, customer satisfaction.

★ ★ ★

Companies are learning that whether they immerse candidates in a full virtual world or not, the fact remains that to attract top talent, there is a growing need to up the candidate experience game.

Forbes has recently put together an HR Leadership Council and here are some of their recent key tips and ideas for securing the best candidates:

"Use Ai wisely, it may not be appropriate in every case and in every organisation. Sometimes, many times, the human touch is what counts!"

"Your organization's reputation permeates candidate decisions. What kind of presence does your organisation have online. Is it compelling, are you monitoring Glassdoor and eNPS public data such as on Comparably.com? If the online presence shows competitive weaknesses then even more challenging to attract and recruit the best talent in the market"

"Learn from Brand and Marketing colleagues to better position HR and the Company's Career opportunities in the market to have the greatest impact. Not enough HR organisations rigorously employ User Experience and Design teams to ensure that a prospective candidate online experience is easy and enjoyable while communicating the key careers messages in a memorable and impactful way"

"Use social media a lot! Organizations now have an opportunity to be visible to many. Candidates are doing their research prior to accepting interviews. They want to know as much as they can. It's key not to be passive and reactive but to dedicate resource to a proactive communication style, keeping HR and Talent attraction on the front foot. Take control of your company's image online!"

Chapter 5

Chief Digital and Technology Officer: future role of CTO/CIO?

For most every organisation now, Technology has become the key driver. Whether to fuel revenue growth, to speed up process and delivery, cut costs, improve performance...without a good and reliable Tech platform most companies will struggle nowadays to compete. So how should the Technology/CTO/CIO group best organise for this?

Most organisations will have an IT Head whose job historically was all about platform maintenance and providing support and enablement to other functions. Many will have graduated and evolved from that historic and siloed way of thinking to appreciate that good IT can of course do more, that it can be an engine of change. And yet, very few companies have their IT Head on the main Board or ExCo.

While Financial Times research has shown that 73% of CEOs interviewed said that Technology was their top priority, yet only 41% of all companies had a CIO or CTO on their main executive Board. And looking specifically at the FTSE 350, only 13% of companies had such a person at that senior level.

CIO magazine conducted a round of interviews to try to understand this reluctance to put the key agenda leader on the main leadership group:

- *"many CIOs and CTOs are the people who get called in to address a specific issue or provide a half yearly update, that's been the history of this role and in many companies that attitude and way of operating still continues"*
- *"some companies try to address this by appointing a non-exec with a Tech background but often that person is not involved in the day-to-day of modern Tech and may be out of touch with the fast pace of change"*
- *"some say that there is a scarcity of good talent, that Tech people may have the technical chops but don't really have the interpersonal skills to engage strategically and regularly at Board level, so they are kept in their department and "wheeled out" when needed!"*

Whatever the arguments that might be put forward, there is no doubt that there *is* a lot of amazing Technology leadership talent and that with the speed that the market place is evolving, so there will be increasing pressure on organisations to find the *right* person to truly be part of the leadership strategy for the company.

Encouragingly, there are nevertheless more businesses waking up to this challenge and the good news is that some have gone even further. They can see the power of Technology but they have also observed just how much value the Tech team can add. They have seen the often constant tension between Tech innovation and commercial innovation and how eg Tech and Marketing departments can be at loggerheads with different views on what are the priorities, conflicts on timing and delivery and teams protecting their turf rather than collaborating openly and transparently.

So the vanguard companies are now creating one core leadership role: the Chief Technology and Digital Officer (sometimes called the Chief Information and Digital Officer), the person who combines the Tech *and* the Commercial leadership into one, who is responsible for all Digital innovation and development and who can prioritise funds and resources to ensure the best leverage of the company's capabilities.

Let's consider some examples of this new and potentially critical leadership role:

Henkel appointed Michael Nilles as Chief Digital & Information Officer. In his role, as a senior member of the ExCo,

> *Nilles is responsible for the combined activities in Integrated Business Solutions (IBS) and digital technologies. We need to shift from digital as a function to digital as an integral business driver. We will overhaul our digital set-up to drive end-to-end customer-centric digitalization with strengthened capabilities in software, in data and analytics, to develop new business-building ideas for additional revenues, efficiency and speed.*

Michael Nilles has also commented on his combined Digital & Tech leadership:

> *As passionate technology innovator, one of my favourite quotes is "Software is eating the world" from Marc Andreessen. This now holds true more than ever and I am super excited to be part of the inflection point. GenAI is disrupting economy & society in a similar magnitude to the Internet - but at lightspeed and my role is to ensure that Henkel captures the opportunity in the most effective way.*

Nike has a Global Chief Digital Information Officer, the role held by Muge Dogan,

> *Moving at the speed of the consumer requires sharpening our ability to sense and serve. Dogan will lead all of Nike's global technology functions across the enterprise* and *with responsibility for accelerating new digital capabilities for Nike.*

Corning appointed Soumya Seetharam as Chief Digital and Information Officer.

> *In this role, Soumya is responsible for leading the strategic direction of Corning's global information technology function and evolving the company's digital footprint. As CDIO, Soumya partners closely with the business unit and functional leaders to evolve our technology capabilities* and *deliver greater value by reshaping Corning's digital outlook in the context of data and analytics, connected ecosystems, the "internet of things," process optimization, and customer service.*

JD Power have established the role of Chief Digital and Technology Officer on their senior leadership team. The first appointment to that position was Bernardo Rodriguez. He initially joined as their Chief Digital Officer, no Tech remit but a focus on e-commerce and digital transformation of their customer engagement. JDP quickly realised that to make this work, then the CDO also had to have the Technology team reporting in:

We needed to create an integrated and joined-up approach to our digital transformation plans and that needed to integrate our commercial and technical approach…we now have a multi-disciplinary team that combines technology with product development…it's a major lever for growth.

One more example comes from Kimberly-Clark, they too have established this CDTO position. Zack Hicks has held that role and he was brought in

To leverage the full potential of technology to accelerate our growth strategy for long term value creation.

Others like PepsiCo, PWC, RICOH, NatWest, Freshfields (global law firm), Gazprom, even the US Navy have all been making similar appointments.

We have to face up to Digital Tech, we need to move at speed, we need to remove as many barriers as possible to do that, we need to break down silos and providing a unified internal organisation structure is a key step in that direction.

As these and other companies have looked into making this hiring, their one key challenge has been whether to hire someone from a commercial background or a Tech background. It's not easy to find someone who genuinely brings both to the table. Most people have started their careers in one area or the other. The Tech person may have graduated in Computer Sciences, had an early career eg in software engineering and then gradually moved into operational, product leadership eventually, perhaps with an MBA extension to their knowledge set to help them adopt a broader commercial approach. Some others may have started eg in Marketing before taking on broader MarTech or wider Tech responsibilities. Some just have a natural aptitude for all this. One such is Atul Bhardwaj who is the CDIO for LEGO Group, an inspirational leader whose energy and enthusiasm and knowhow makes him a natural business leader leveraging early career tech knowhow and subsequent broader commercial experience.

But whoever we look at it is clear that winning companies do need to actively consider how to best organise to exploit the bewildering range of new Tech opportunities.

© marketoonist.com

Chapter 6

Technology vs People – finding the balance: a new operating model for the 21st century

In the preceding chapters, we've been examining the power and potential of new technologies, how they can be the key engines of growth and performance improvement, how they can be game-changers in almost every business sector and for almost any organisation that has the will and desire to leverage what Tech can do.

But, in all this, what about People? Where's the balance, how can we ensure that the rush to automate does not do so at the expense of people's jobs, lives and well-being? How can we try to find a balance, a way forward that embraces both Technology *and* People, a way of operating that respects the individual and acknowledges that in fact: *it is people who make the difference.*

In this regards, a new Operating and Business Model is being increasingly considered and debated. It's a model for the 2020's and beyond. It represents a reappraisal about how best to orchestrate and manage a company. It's a sea change that could be become the most accepted way of managing a business, but it is a game-changer too and perhaps those companies who are in the vanguard of adopting and embracing it will be the very best placed to be the winners and success stories of the future.

This "new" business model is the "3Ps" model: the triple bottom line framework:

People   Planet   Profit

This was first devised by a Professor John Elkington of University College, London. It's intended as a framework for business governance and management and it has never been more relevant than in today's complex, challenging and fast-changing environment.

The aim is that a company would report *with equal emphasis* on these 3Ps. It would set KPi (key performance indicators) to measure and monitor. The idea being that each element is reinforcing the other to create a virtuous circle.

For example, it should no longer be enough to talk just about shareholder value and to justify all corporate behaviours along that line. Yes, that will always remain critical, but surely it can no longer be seen in isolation. And more importantly, it should be evaluated alongside and with equal weight to the impact on the other Ps of People and Planet.

It might for example be the lowest cost, best shareholder value solution to build a new factory in a low cost low regulation environment. But if that might lead to higher emissions, or more carbon footprint or damage to the planet then that can no longer be the right answer. Investing shareholders have to learn to accept this "new normal", that the optimal solution may not be the lowest cost /highest Profit option.

That will of course be difficult! The 3P's is looking to overturn not just decades but centuries of embedded thinking about how to run a company. You do it for profit, of course!? But now we are trying to challenge that, to start a new dialogue in the business community. A dialogue that says that other things now have become increasingly critical. Protecting our planet is surely a "must-have" way of thinking and operating. Looking after employee welfare and the impact of what we do on the people around us, how can we nowadays just ignore that or ride roughshod over that justified by a zealous focus on profit alone.

This is a discussion that is gaining increasing momentum especially in North America and Western Europe.

"Earth provides enough to satisfy every man's needs, but not every man's greed."
– Gandhi

"Sustainable development is a fundamental break that's going to reshuffle the entire deck. There are companies today that are going to dominate the future simply because they understand that"
– Francois-Henri Pinault, CEO of Kering (Pinault, Printemps, Redoute)

"A coalition of twenty-one UK universities collectively managing more than £5bn in cash and investments has warned banks and asset managers they are ready to move funds to greener institutions unless they accelerate their net zero investments and halt financing of new fossil fuel projects."

"The Discovery Group [$13bn market cap] was founded with a core purpose to make people healthier and to enhance and protect their lives. Our shared value business model, which seeks to drive positive behaviour change to deliver better outcomes for individuals, our business and wider society, is aligned with the aims to drive a healthy, safe, resilient and sustainable society"
– Adrian Gore, CEO of Discovery Inc.

"Farmers Inc. is committed to operating in a way that positively impacts our customers, our employees and communities by incorporating Environmental, Social and Governance (ESG) considerations into our business. We are honored to become the first U.S.-based insurer to sign the Principles for Sustainable Insurance (PSI) and hope to amplify the impact of our efforts by inspiring others in the insurance industry to follow our example."
– Raul Vargas, President and CEO of Farmers Group Inc.

"This supersedes political parties, race, creed, religion, it doesn't matter. If we do not solve the environment, we're all damned."
– Elon Musk

"People should have values, so by extension, a company should. And one of the things you do is give back. So how do you give back? We give back through our work in the environment, in running the company on renewable energy. We give back in job creation."
– Tim Cook, CEO of Apple

"The brands that will be big in the future will be those that tap into the social changes that are taking place."
– Sir Michael Perry, Chairman of Centrica PLC

Sustainability is no longer about doing less harm. It's about doing more good. Progress is impossible without change"
– Jochen Zeitz, CEO of Harley-Davidson

Encouragingly, the above quotations do show that the wider business community is taking this 3Ps debate seriously. Though of course we do wonder how much of that is just paying lip-service to the ideal, versus actually and meaningfully doing something fundamental and substantive.

The 3Ps "originator" John Elkington and his team have sought to respond to the challenge about what's really required to succeed, what do these 3Ps actually mean for an organisation and how can we evaluate and measure how well a company is really doing?

The following sets out a questionnaire and guide. Elkington suggests that "by considering these questions and taking steps to enhance your social impact, you can become more responsible and sustainable, benefiting both society and your bottom line."

1. People – Questions to Assess Your Impact on People
Here are some questions to ask to assess whether your business is helping People, which is one of the three bottom lines of the people, planet, profit framework:

1. *How does our business impact our employees and their families?*
2. *What is our approach to diversity, equity, and inclusion, and how do we ensure that our employees are treated fairly and equitably?*
3. *How do we contribute to the well-being of the communities where we operate, and do we have any negative impacts on those communities?*
4. *What steps do we take to ensure the safety and well-being of our customers?*

5. *How do we ensure that our suppliers and partners adhere to ethical and responsible business practices?*

6. *Do we have a charitable giving program, and how do we select the causes we support?*

7. *How do we measure and report on our social impact, and do we have any programs in place to continually improve our social impact?*

2. Planet – Questions to Assess Your Impact on the Planet

These questions can help you evaluate your impact on the Planet and identify areas where you can improve your environmental impact.

1. *How do our operations impact the environment, including our carbon footprint, waste generation, and water usage?*

2. *Do we have a plan to reduce our environmental impact, and how are we tracking progress against our goals?*

3. *How do we ensure that our products and services are environmentally responsible and sustainable?*

4. *Do we have a policy to reduce our use of non-renewable resources and transition to renewable resources where possible?*

5. *How do we measure and report on our environmental impact, and do we have any programs in place to continually improve our environmental impact?*

6. *Do we have any initiatives in place to engage our customers and employees in environmental responsibility?*

3. Profit – Questions to Assess Your impact on Your Profit

These questions can help businesses evaluate their financial performance and identify areas where they can improve their profitability, in a sustainable way.

1. *How are we measuring our financial performance, and what metrics are we using to track profitability?*

2. *What is our strategy for achieving financial sustainability, and how do we balance financial performance with social and environmental responsibility?*

3. *Do we have a plan to grow our revenue and increase profitability over the long term?*

4. *How do we manage financial risks, such as economic downturns or changes in market conditions?*

5. *Are we effectively managing costs to optimize our profitability while minimizing negative impacts on people and the planet?*

6. *Are we making investments in sustainable technologies and processes that will enhance our long-term profitability while also improving our social and environmental impact?*

It's clear that a growing number of companies are at least grappling with these questions and are publicly committed to the 3Ps - many now use the label "ESG" to showcase what they are doing.

ESG stands for Environment Social Responsibility and Good Governance. And ESG is becoming the most widely used term to capture some of the key elements of this 3Ps approach. In fact, Listed companies with more than 500 employees or more than £500m of turnover, under the guidance of the UK Financial Reporting Council (FRC), are now formally required to disclose specific ESG-related information. We also see this in the EU and the USA. In the EU, there has been a raft of new regulations, including the Corporate Sustainability Reporting Directive where most companies with operations in the EU will be required to publish regular reports on their sustainable activities and a rolling timetable based on size of business about their plans and target deliverables. It's estimated that some 50,000 companies across the EU will be impacted by these regulations as they get rolled out and expanded to cover any organisation potentially with any sales activity in an EU country. Also in the EU especially the repercussions for non-compliance are significant with the threat of large fines and other sanctions.

However most of the emphasis in ESG to date has all been around energy usage, carbon emissions and path to "net zero". So "Planet" gets good focus and emphasis. So far much less activity and focus on People and the impact on them, other than targets around diversity and inclusion at senior levels in the company.

So progress being made and now there's further momentum with the development of "B-Corporation" certification.

There are a number of research and investment firms who monitor and measure how companies are responding to the ESG guidelines. The likes of Bloomberg, MSCI, Refinitiv all publish scorecards and reports. But perhaps the most influential measure and best regarded is the B-Corp standard.

B-Corp was started in the USA as B Lab and as a not-for-profit to encourage an ESG/Sustainable approach to business activity and investment. They have gone on to develop a scoring system of up to 100 points reviewing public statements, annual reports, carbon footprint, corporate sustainability measures, board structure, remuneration and bonus targets to then develop and publish an annual score and rating. According to MSCI: "Companies are concerned about how investors and people perceive their ESG behaviour and their actions about the environment, how they look after their people, their diversity goals. Fund management teams now look at ESG scores to determine investment attractiveness".

B-Corp has been at the forefront encouraging this. They audit and certify companies for their social and environmental performance, accountability, and transparency. There are now more than 10,000 certified "B Corps" across 77 countries and 153 industries. They all subscribe to a common goal: *to transform the global economy to benefit all people, communities, and the planet.*

Within this business community, there is significant publicity around the top 5% of all B Corps worldwide for their sustainable business practices:

> *This year's Best for the World B-Corp companies are operating at the very top of their class, excelling in creating positive impact for their stakeholders, including their workers, communities, customers, and the environment. These are the sort of companies employees now prefer to work for.*

Chris Biggs is the Senior Client Relationship Director at NatWest Bank and he has commented:

> *We are seeing an ever-increasing proportion of our corporate clients now developing credible, quantifiable and often very socially impactful ESG strategies and a number are now going further to have their actions ratified externally through the B-Corp certification process and whether officially B-Corp certified or not, an ability to articulate a commitment to an ESG strategy and plan has become a key part of what any company needs to do if it is to tender to win new contracts, keep existing customers, motivate employees and attract new talent.*

In this context then, a positive case study:

Baringa is a global management consultancy, operating across 15 countries, employing c. 2500 people. Their mission: "We set out to build the world's most trusted consulting firm – creating lasting impact for clients and *pioneering a positive, people-first way of working.*"

Baringa talk about *People first*, then Planet and then Profit. Their view, if we get People and Planet right then we'll be doing the right things and Profit will follow.

The way they approach this is to carry the torch for "corporate kindness".

"Does kindness in business pay? We believe so. For us, kindness makes good business sense, it's an enduring tenet of business success. Businesses that organise themselves in this way will be the ones who succeed."

Baringa go on to say that kindness for them is not something "fluffy", but it's something that informs everything they do, whether in difficult but honest conversations with clients or the way we interact with their people. Especially they are finding that new recruits have an "infectious enthusiasm" for making the world a better place and to attract and retain the best talent they need to adapt and embrace but also show that this is the most critical part of the way they will work.

"At Baringa, in our client work we are seeing that the more conscious and environmentally aware companies are thriving and in fact people are willing to pay a premium for such products and services. We have done research that shows that 36% of people interviewed prefer to buy products and services from companies with strong environment credentials and c. 80% of business execs interviewed said they would in the future expect to purchase all their materials and services from companies that could demonstrate they are environmentally friendly.

One of Baringa's clients is the American retailer Patagonia. They have seen revenues grow by 4x in the past 10 yrs as they have demonstrably upped their ESG credentials:

It's no question that Patagonia has revolutionised the ESG world. When you hear "Patagonia", you don't just envision the outdoor clothing line: you envision social goodness. As one article headline writes, "the more Patagonia rejects consumerism, the more the brand sells.

The company garnered national attention for its innovative business model, transcending the traditional division between environmentalism and capitalism. Through fair labour practices, sustainable production, and philanthropy, Patagonia has become the epitome of an ideal stock for ESG investors. In spite of all its considerations that may compromise its low costs, Patagonia maintains a 10% profit margin that beats other publicly traded apparel companies.

Patagonia trailblazed a new model of capitalism, effectively advancing the world of ESG investing.

The company sells more than $1 billion worth of outdoor apparel each year, valuing the company at around $3 billion. Hence, it's almost paradoxical to acknowledge that Patagonia is also one of the world's most sustainable and ethical multinational corporations.

To take things further, the family-owned business recently broke headlines once again by giving away its ownership of Patagonia to the Patagonia Purpose Trust (a uniquely curated trust) and Holdfast Collective (a non-profit). This ensures that the company's profits of around $100 million per year are dedicated to combatting ecological crises such as biodiversity loss and climate change.

Among U.S adults who were already aware of Patagonia, data from CivicScience shows that 42% are "more likely to purchase their products" given that the company has essentially been donated to fight against the global climate crisis.

One thing is clear: we can't go back to an historic 20th century business and operating model. Time has moved on, things will never be the same again.

From the MTV nominated best song by Mel C of the Spice Girls:

Things will never be the same again
It's just the beginning it's not the end
Things will never be the same again
It's not a secret anymore
Now we've opened up the door
Starting tonight and from now on
We'll never, never be the same again

"You must be the change you wish to see in the world."
– Mahatma Gandhi

Chapter 7

The Chief Heart Officer

Technology vs People? What more can an organisation do to try to find the appropriate balance, to make sure as new Technology gets adopted and implemented that People are not left behind, but are instead engaged, involved, integrated, key members of any transformation process and embraced for what they can *continue* to contribute and accomplish within the organisation.

The focus on looking after People has become even more challenging with the advent of remote, flexible, "work from home" ways of being employed. This has very quickly become a new norm and yet it makes looking after People even more complicated when you hardly see them except on an occasional videocall. How engage, manage and motivate and inspire a remote workforce? How build a team spirit among people you only see on ZOOM? How create a buzz, a culture, an esprit de corps?

Some argue that maybe it doesn't matter? So long as the job gets done then should we care, we can manage against specific tasks, check on progress, make sure that things get completed, ask people to deliver on budgets and reporting and on time. And, in the short term, that can probably work ok, and we can start to think, hey this remote working is cool, people get to spend more time with their family, no commuting and travel stress, more time in the day to be productive?

But, there are of course longer term consequence. People can work to do their job, but just that, and begin to care less about the company they're working for. Fill in the forms, do the numbers, send in the reports, get the monthly pay check. Ok, job done and then what, do I care? And does this also lead to a lack of connection, an absence of community, no sharing of ideas, gossip, fun, laughter, it becomes just a job, could be for any company or just any organisation?

Research over many years has consistently shown one key thing that distinguishes those companies who are successful, and those that are not, those that survive and renew and build success sustainably for the long term, who provide *enduring employment prospects* as well as positive shareholder value. That key thing? It's companies that have an engaged, enthusiastic, "I love my company" culture, companies where employees are committed and engaged and ready to go the extra mile, where they look forward to their job, to the social interaction as part of their doing their work, "the people I work with are also friends", "I learn from the people around me, learning on the job, being guided by team and colleagues", "it's that casual interaction when passing in the corridor or sharing lunch in the canteen that builds our mutual commitment, a trust in each other, a wanting to make 2+2 =5".

The Boston Consulting Group, BCG, has done some ground-breaking research in this area. They were looking at the underpinning reasons that lie behind a company's long-term success, why do some continue to do well, while others fall by the wayside?

What they found is that there are three key factors: *Head, Hearts and Hands. And the most important and hardest to achieve was the Heart.* What did they mean?

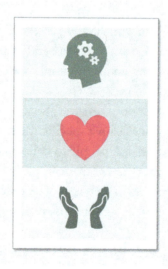

In their research they examined in detail more than 100 companies globally. They found that those who were the long-term successes scored highly on 3 key areas. A great strategy and vision (the *"Head"*), passionate employee engagement (the *"Heart"*) and having the skills and resources to deliver (the*"Hands"*). They discovered that most companies could register a good score on the Head, they did have a credible strategy and vision. But they found that many companies failed crucially on the *Heart*, they really hadn't managed to engage the workforce, there was no underlying commitment and enthusiasm for the organisation they were working for, they did the job but they didn't much care, so long as the pay check arrived. This lack of *Heart* seemed to be the key deciding factor in the BCG research.

This 3 H's model sounds straightforward, seems simple, surely that is all just good business management and planning. But time and again, many of the BCG researched companies had failed to fully appreciate the amount of effort required to build that engaged workforce culture, that *Heart* and spirit and what might be needed to make it happen.

As BCG dug deeper, they found companies like Nationwide Building Society, LV Insurance, 3M, Zappos, Virgin, Red Hat, Adobe, Home Depot, Procter & Gamble, South West Airlines and others leading the way in their *Heart* scores and in their employee engagement (their "EE"). And described this simple formula:

Employee Engagement = Customer Happiness = Market Success

Virgin

At Virgin, we do not put the customer first. It's Virgin employees who are the company's top priority. That may sound like a decades-old business wisdom, but it works. If the person who works at your company is 100 per cent proud of the organisation and they're treated well, they're going to be happy and they're going to make the customers pleased too.

– Interview with Richard Branson

Gary Hamel

Harvard Business School Professor: "To put it bluntly, the most important task for any manager today is to still create a work environment that inspires exceptional contribution and that merits an outpouring of passion, imagination and initiative.

Red Hat

I have never seen a company of this size where the people are so passionate about wanting their company to do well"
– CIO.com

Zappos

We're proud that our employees say they feel inspired. A culture that keeps the fun and is dedicated to making customers happy all fit in with the Zappos approach. When you get the company culture right, great customer service and a great company will happen on its own.
– Interview with former CEO Tony Hsieh

Southwest Airlines

We are always looking to engage and communicate to our employees in a way that will make them feel part here of a unified team. We want our people to be convinced of a larger common goal and to be excited by that. In that way we believe they will feel empowered to go the extra mile to make our customers happy"

★ ★ ★

People-first, will we now start to see more of that? Perhaps now more than ever there's a need to redouble efforts to secure employee welfare and well-being, to make sure they feel valued and supported and to show the company cares. Perhaps now is the time to see a more compassionate people strategy and approach, a plan that embraces the "people first" commitment described at Virgin and Red Hat and others.

Vayner Media (a $150m digital marketing agency) has been a pioneer. They appointed a *"Chief Heart Officer"*. Claude Silver has that role at Vayner, and her mantra is: "people will give you their hearts when you acknowledge, nurture and inspire theirs in return".

Claude Silver explains how she sees this role as follows:

It used to be that a successful business leader had to show they were tough. Jack Welch, long time CEO of GE, would infamously claim to fire the underperforming 10% each and every year. Steve Jobs of Apple fame had a reputation for being blunt, he was known to have little patience with people, his employees used to dread getting in an elevator with him, not a "people person". But our passion here at Vayner is to build an organisation in a nice way, honey over vinegar.

Silver goes on to describe the way she works:

As Chief Heart Officer, I work for 800 human being, 800 souls. I am in touch with the heartbeat of every single person in the company. My role is to infuse the business with empathy and purpose. We want this company to be a place where people can find a home. Now more than ever is a time to provide a connecting and emotional landscape where our people can feel realistic and optimistic.

A key approach that Silver promotes is mentorship. "For us it's essential, it's the glue that keeps us together, informed about what's going on, a sounding board, an advisor, a friend, a guide. Every single person is given the responsibility to mentor another and some take on that charge for a number of people. And we measure that, 360 feedback, how many interactions, quality, would you recommend that person as a mentor to others, all done anonymously, but still checked and evaluated to make sure we deliver on this promise."

Another advocate of the "Chief Heart Officer" role has been Dionne Kress who is the CHO at US Haulage company Port X Logistics, an organisation that aims to utilise a core mix of new tech and culture. Talking about her role:

I have often been asked about my role as the Chief Heart Officer. People are curious about what I do and how I help the organization and people achieve their purpose and goals.

First, it is important to know the title/position was inspired by Claude Silver. My role is quite similar. I touch the lives and hearts of every single person within Port X Logistics across four states and five offices. My purpose is to serve the people; guiding, coaching, supporting and collaborating with each one of them about life and work.

I have always been inspired by people who want to learn, grow and be a better version of themselves. It is easy to sit idle and wish you could achieve or do more with your life or career. It's the individual who puts in the effort who truly inspires me. They recognize their ability to realize their greatness and readily engage with me to do the work.

My role is not to change people. I believe people already have everything they need. They have simply sometimes overlooked or underestimated their natural born gifts and talents. They have been influenced by life experiences causing them maybe to self-doubt and have feeling of uncertainty. I serve as a guide who reintroduces them to who they already are. I instil a sense of confidence and self-assuredness that helps them get unstuck.

I coach each person to write their personal story. It has been said, if everyone in the organization can write their best personal and professional book, the company thrives. This is how you change lives AND enhance a company's heart. I help each person to begin the process of writing their book and creating their legacy.

In its simplicity I take care of the people. I show them heart, empathy, love and compassion. I let them know they matter and have a significant contribution to make. A contribution to their own legacy and to the organization.

Today, as we face more questions than answers, I feel like the beacon of light in the storm for some. Supporting and guiding each person as they attempt to navigate rough waters and uncertain tides. I have served as the web, connecting lines of communication with each member of the team. This has resulted in strengthened collaborative efforts, team support, and renewed sense of comradery.

Simply put my role is to take care of the people. I feel like I have a cool title and certainly my dream job. I love what I do every day. I guide people toward remembering who they really are without all the self-doubt, judgment and internal criticism.

If every organization had a CHO people would have a very different work experience all together and more organizations would prosper in uncertain times.

Further research on building and nurturing People has come from The Centre for Agile Leadership ("CAL"):

"There's no doubt that in these more uncertain times, the role of the HR department and team becomes ever more challenging and demanding. There's no established off the shelf policy so HR leaders have to become more innovative and open-minded about how they can best engage their workforce and keep them motivated. We might expect to see more roles dedicated to looking after the heart of the organisation."

And for example, Bupa, the health care company, appointed a Chief Wellbeing Officer in Fiona Adshead who worked tirelessly to build a more people-first culture and agenda (and eg developed Bupa's dedicated "EWP", their employee wellbeing programme.)

And a number of companies in the CAL research have it seems at least been discussing making similar appointments.

"What might once have been deemed outlandish job titles now represent a response to this new wave of Tech and the threat of automation."

To achieve these high levels of Employee engagement ("EE"), winning the *"Heart"* of the workforce, nowadays requires a sophisticated and committed programme. This is especially so in trying to build EE across a hybrid working workforce who perhaps will only occasionally meet in person. And it will need to be proactively led by HR and backed by the Board and ExCo.

It was of course never just about buying football tables and pinball machines and a few comfy chairs!

Recent PWC research spotlighted 7 global corporations who are starting to build a more effective "EE" environment. They are: Google, Microsoft, Asana, Accenture, Nike, Expedia and Netflix.

Accenture is a good example. They have approached this from a health and wellbeing perspective. They have developed 4 key aspects: (i) heart and lungs, (ii) wrist, core and spine, (iii) nutrition, hydration and digestion and (iv) sleep and mental health. They look to provide regular employee health assessments, plus gym memberships, health coaches and counselling services. At Expedia, everyone gets a wellness allowance of c. $1000, at Netflix, they are big on things like time off for new parents (up to one year's paid leave), plus unlimited time-off for personal matters eg family emergency, child care etc.

But while health care and wellbeing are certainly key components, the research shows they don't go far enough. There needs to be a more complete, more holistic programme which captures *all* the core learnings described in this chapter and pushes to really make a difference, for everyone.

In summary we can define the following "Employee Engagement /EE" framework, with 7 core items. All of this adds up to a valuable way to truly build employee engagement and win over the Heart of the workforce in 2025 and beyond:

Work:life balance
Communication
Positive workspace
Health and mindfulness
Time-outs
Mentor
Reward

A few words on each:

Work:life balance is oft quoted as something an employer commits to, but of course it needs actions not words. The Netflix example is a good illustration, time off no questions asked, *"we trust you"*. That declaration of trust is key. The time-off can of course be monitored and some may abuse the goodwill but research by Netflix has shown that any abuse is negligible and that people *can* and *should* be trusted to do their job well while enjoying some discretion on when the work gets done. Trust, give and take, supporting people to live their lives, find time for their families…all that makes a difference.

Communication: sounds obvious but how often is communication done personally, done well, done with care and attention. A very successful UK venture has been Simply Business, they employ some 500 people, the company is doing very well, now part of Travellers Inc but very much retaining its independent spirit, it has built an extraordinary culture and team spirit, has won awards for best place to work, is a highly sought-after employer, and one thing they are known for is their clear, regular, honest all employee comms and updates with town hall meetings every week led by their CEO. Even with remote/hybrid working, this communication has continued, seamlessly. It is enormously valued, most all employees join in, there is open dialogue and Q&A. It works and people end the meeting genuinely feeling uplifted and inspired.

Yes, it helps that the company is 500 and not 5000 but no matter the size of the corporation, that sort of communication plan can still be done on a team, country, department and function basis. No excuse for it not to happen.

Positive workspace: for some it's easy and pleasant to work from home or work remotely. For others, they may not have a quiet convenient comfortable workspace. It may be hard for them to be productive, internet signals and connectivity may be poor. There may be noise and distraction. So efforts to help employees manage this, support to ensure they can find a positive remote working environment, setting up pods in the office with formal social distancing, funding good home computer equipment, providing IT/technical support and back-up, easily accessed and available 24/7, just doing everything possible to make an employee as productive and also as looked after as can be.

Health & Mindfulness: The Accenture example described above is helpful. One company I work with enables all their senior employees to take a week out once every two years to attend a mindfulness course. One week to focus on self, me time, reconnect with what's important to you. It's a course that's highly respected and valued and is a core part of their culture of learning and sharing

Time outs: just as important as occasional mindfulness retreats are more regular day-to day time-outs. If we are in an office, we wander over to the kitchen or coffee area or water cooler or we step outside for a cigarette or a walk round the block or a trip to Starbucks and usually with a colleague or two to share ideas, chat through worries and anxieties, talk generally about what's working, what's not, what's good, what's bad. It's the classic office time-out. But in a remote, hybrid-working world not so easy. But such letting off steam, taking time-out is essential to employee well-being, to productivity, to building that shared culture and engagement. So some companies are now asking their employees to take one hour each day to do that. It may be by Zoom or Slack, it may be eg in 15 minute chunks of time, but if the company embraces this, makes it positive, values the experience, encourages this to happen, tasks team leaders to get their teams to do this, in two's and three's, it can still be effective.

Mentoring: the example above from Claude Silver at Vayner Media is a good illustration to encourage employee care and attention

Reward: this seems perhaps so obvious yet again it is something so rarely seen; reward those employees who do go the extra mile on all this. It could be part of their bonus. It could be a separate payment. But it's the symbolism, the recognition that those who do this are making a significant contribution to the company's long term and sustainable success.

★ ★ ★

Companies talk eagerly about "it's people who make the difference". But often that mantra trips off the tongue without being clearly understood, lost amid an array of other initiatives and priorities, relegated to an occasional hour of time or quarterly review it cannot make an impact.

Putting *EE* at the Heart of the organisation

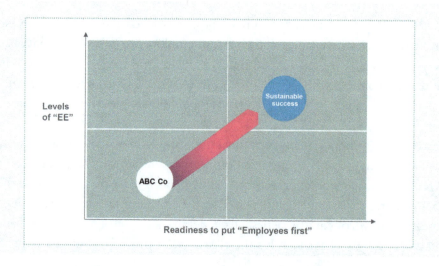

As we can see from the case examples described here, it requires a very determined effort. It does mean asking some very far-reaching questions: do we formally adopt an *"employees first"* strategy, what should we be doing to drive that, what kind of investment in time and energy will it take, are we willing and ready to *truly* do that, do we believe in our hearts that it will pay back, do we believe it will be the foundation of a winning formula and lasting sustainable and renewable success?

Every organisation should be asking: "where are we on our EE /Heart effectiveness today and are we ready to truly embrace that ideal?"

As summarised in a recent Forbes article: "the truth is that high levels of employee engagement don't happen by accident. To the contrary, organizations who have achieved it have done so as a result of deep commitment and intention. It requires significant effort, but the benefits are tremendous. What's it worth to have an organization full of highly motivated and engaged workers who even in a dislocated remote working world still feel great about the work they do and the teams they work with? Priceless…."

Chapter 8

People, People, People

Recent research from PWC has shown that the 63% of HR Heads now say that "employee engagement", nurturing and looking after their People, has become their core focus, to ensure the employee base feels motivated and committed, confident and also comfortable working for the company. 47% of CEOs now say they are putting this as a top 3 agenda item to drive the success and sustainability of their business.

With all the focus on ESG and discussion about the 3Ps, many companies are actively reappraising their people strategies, benchmarking the best practices on how others are doing and identifying new priorities. How make their organisation as the most relevant and appealing, how make sure that the company best presents its core values, how ensure it meets expectations around new ways of working, culture norms, the environment, how best showcase its credentials as a "best place to work", how ensure that the feedback on the now very public Glassdoor reviews is positive and closer to 4 stars rather than 2.

With high levels of demand for talent and still relatively low unemployment rates, the challenge to excel in successfully managing people is becoming ever more critical. What's more, we now have a tech-savvy, digitally-expectant workforce, with GenZ now making up more than 20% of the employee base. We see their increased focus around the environment, around sustainability, challenging what is the organisation doing in that regard? There are heightened expectations around diversity and inclusion, factors which are now very measurable and visible. What is the company doing for disabled people, what are the policies around remote or hybrid working, does the company support paternity leave? It's a new set of challenges and ways of working and to succeed an organisation has to respond.

Measure your eNPS

eNPS, employee net promoter score, is a core tool for measuring just how effective HR policies and procedures are for building and nurturing employee welfare.

Before getting into that detail, it's helpful to just remind ourselves of the benefits of better employee engagement, on putting employees first, and why that is so important:

- *Sasser & Reichheld at Harvard found that "employee engagement" is the key to driving market success. Their research showed employee engagement significantly increases customer loyalty and can increase profits by as much as 25%.*
- *McKinsey found that c.70% of all customer buying decisions are based on how well they are treated by the organisation and its employees.*
- *Gallup Consulting discovered that high employee engagement companies grow their earnings per share ("EPS") at a faster rate of 28% while low employee engagement firms experienced an average EPS decline rate of 9.4%.*
- *The Center for Human Resources Strategy at Rutgers University found that businesses with highly engaged workforces were on average 3.4x more effective financially in terms of sales and revenue growth*
- *Peakon and Hays research has shown that "highly engaged companies have 37% fewer sick days, 30% higher productivity levels and 2.5x better customer satisfaction scores."*

And we have already talked about companies like Nationwide Building Society, LV Insurance, 3M, Zappos, Virgin, Red Hat, Adobe, Home Depot, Procter & Gamble, South West Airlines and others are leading the way in this respect. They are showing that:

Employee Engagement = Customer Happiness = Market Success.

eNPS is a way to measure this. It has been adopted by many large corporations in the USA and is becoming increasingly used in Europe and Asia. It measures very simply just one key metric:

- *On a scale of 0 to 10, how likely is it that you would recommend our company as a place to work?*

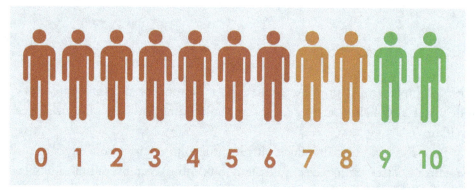

- *Promoters*: give the score 9 or 10 and are "extremely likely" to recommend
- *Passively Satisfied*: they give a score of 7 or 8 and are neutral. They're not likely to recommend but they're satisfied with the experience
- *Detractors*: give a score of 0 to 6 and are not all likely to recommend.

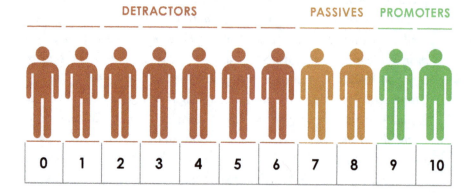

One of the early adopters of eNPS was Apple. They started using it in their stores to identify those employees who were the most positive, the most enthusiastic about the organisation, those who were giving scores of 9 or 10. Why, what was it that was motivating them, how was that translating into their behaviour with their customers in the stores, what did they do differently, what impact did it have on sales and customer feedback, what could be learned and so passed on to other employees?

Of course the scoring is all very well, but the real value comes in the follow-ups. The learning around the scoring is that it can change and change quickly. A "Promoter" today with a 9 or even a 10 score can quickly become a detractor if the company changes materially in how it operates or behaves towards its staff. So these scores need a regular monitor and check.

Equally if someone is a "Detractor" today, then important to understand why is that: "what is the key thing that's stopping you promoting the company, what's holding you back, what needs to change?

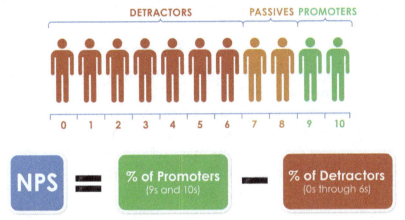

eNPS scores are now often publicly available so it can sometimes be impossible to hide a poor score performance. Equally those with high eNPS want to promote and highlight to provide for outside investors and stakeholders an additional and insightful perspective on just how well they are performing and *the underlying* potential of the corporation.

Comparably.com brilliantly captures a lot of eNPS data and it's possible to compare and contrast performance of one company vs another and especially discover who's doing well in an industry sector:

eNPS for example US Insurers		
Company (listed by size of revenue)	eNPS score	Culture (rating A to D)
1. Prudential	+44	A
2. State Farm	- 8	C
3. Allstate	+9	B
4. Berkshire Hathaway Insurance	+40	A
5. Liberty Mutual	+28	A
9. AIG	-45	D
13. Chubb	+30	B
15. CNA Insurance	-57	D

"Involved in the community and genuinely caring"
"Everyone here is friends with each other."
– Berkshire Hathaway +40

"The leadership has no clue"
"Everyone lives in fear"
"Need to learn how to retain people"
"They pay me and the check clears"
– AIG -45

There is clearly significant disparity! between the likes of Berkshire Hathaway in comparison to AIG. One has built a solid, committed, engaged employee community. While the other has failed, with employees only there "because they pay me and the check clears"!

We can also consider some other case study examples where eNPS has become a key internal indicator as to the company's well-being:

LV Insurance

Debbie Kennedy, as Director, made the following comment about the organisation:

> *Insurance should be more than just about providing cover and paying claims. It should also help provide emotional and practical support at times like these, to our customers and to everyone who works for us.*

What lay behind these kind words?

LV is one of the UK's largest insurance companies with more than 5 million customers and offering a range of personal and life insurance, pension and savings.

It has been voted "best loved insurer" 5 yrs running, it has been rated by Moneywise as "most trusted insurer" and has won best life and pensions provider 8x by Moneyfacts.

Former CEO Richard Rowney talked in these terms:

Our goal is to help customers, members and colleagues feel more confident about life and more confident in us. We have a strong customer service ethos. They are at the centre of what we do. We know we have to keep evolving and improving and taking advantage of new technologies in a way that's helpful to us and to our customers and not to replace the tried and tested. eNPS measures are very helpful guidelines on how well we're doing. Companies like Amazon and John Lewis set the bar for what customers expect and we need to keep investing and building. So we are always trying to improve our employee experience, recognising that great customer experience starts from the inside out.

Current CEO, David Hynam reinforces this employee well-being message:

I try hard to treat others with fairness & kindness, and to have empathy. I believe that successful business outcomes are because of, and not in conflict with, doing that. I know that having a leadership role is a privilege - to serve colleagues, customers and members.

I passionately believe that we must celebrate inclusion & diversity in the workplace & in society. I was the very first signatory to the Government backed pledge to champion Diversity and Inclusion in business. As CEO, I was very proud to launch the 'Be You' public commitment to diversity and the inclusion pledge that 'Everyone's Welcome'. By working with amazing colleagues, I'm proud to have been recognised over many years for being a leading voice driving."

LV have a generous array of employee benefits to help their staff engage. Everyone is eligible for the LV bonus scheme, all are able to participate in the pension plan up to a 14% matched contribution, there are coffee cards for new joiners, healthcare, holidays for top-performing employees and their families, weekly thank you cards and gift vouchers with more than 23,000 sent out in the last year (workforce of 5000), flexible working, crowdsourcing /funding plans for new ideas, a customer leadership academy…a lot of effort going in to make employees feel valued and motivated.

David Hynam has also been a keen advocate of "walking the talk". He talks about wanting to: "build the culture to make everybody around feel welcome and looking to help each other. We like to encourage that especially.

There's lots of communication at LV as well and I expect all my mangers to be out there walking around talking to people. We care here about our staff and members and it can be seen constantly".

Nationwide

Nationwide has over 15 million members/customers across the UK. It is the second largest UK Bank in terms of consumer savings and mortgages with assets of more than £200bn.

It has consistently been ranked among in the top 5 best big companies to work for, has been voted No.1 UK Bank by Business Insider, has been the Which? Banking Brand of the Year and described in a consumer survey as: "the most trustworthy, straightforward, helpful and friendly Bank" (Good Housekeeping).

Joe Garner, an ex P&G person, was the CEO there for 7 years. He talked in this way about how Nationwide is organised and managing continuous change:

> We have a mission to build a trusted community of customers and employees… customers stay with us because of our record of outstanding customer services… that's being given every day by our staff and it is at the heart of what we do.
>
> Underpinning our success is our recognition of our employees. There is a sense of Pride that runs through the whole organisation so that our employees want to serve our customers in the best possible way.

Nationwide gets an A score on its positive culture and a +38 eNPS. "We have really creative, motivated people on our team. I like working with people who are invested and have great ideas they are willing to stand up for."

The business has established a range of employee benefits which include time off for local charity volunteer work, everyone eligible for the pension scheme and a minimum 4% employer contribution, free healthcare for employees and their family, flexible working including part time, flexi time, school term time only and home /remote working, minimum 24 days holiday for all, vouchers /employee rewards each week for work well-done, celebrations of employees "who go the extra mile" with their stories published for all to read, long service awards…employees feel valued and their efforts recognised.

And as the key that keeps all these good things in place, Joe Garner is a very good example of a business leader who walks the talk. Joe talks about the "courage to care", the desire to do the right thing by staff and customers, the goal of building a caring environment where staff can flourish and change can be delivered. He cascaded these messages throughout the organisation all the time. He also held regular "town hall" meetings where progress is shared and success celebrated. He was proud to say: "there's a level of openness and transparency at Nationwide that I've not seen anywhere else."

South West Airlines

SWA Chairman and former CEO Gary Kelly continues to provide updates and share his thoughts and gives his thanks to our Employees, the heroes on the frontline.

Founded in 1967, SWA has become the largest domestic US airline. Revenues exceed $21bn. They have now recorded their 45th consecutive year of profitability (while some once rival carriers have either merged or reported continued trading difficulties). The share price is up 3x over the past 5yrs.

SWA has been named for the 24th straight year as one of Forbes Most Admired Companies. They are consistently ranked No. 1 Airline for customer satisfaction, have been voted "one of the best employers to work for" in Glassdoor polls for the 9th year running, named in the top 100 for Corporate Responsibility and voted best US Airline for 8 consecutive years. SWA gets an A+ on Culture and a +68 eNPS.

This is a company that completely subscribes to the mantra that employee engagement drives customer satisfaction = market success. In the company's annual report, the first thing that Gary Kelly says is: "I want to thank our people for our exceptional results and congratulate them. Our strong financial

performance provides the cash flow to continue to reward our employees…
and so deliver more value to our customers". SWA shares its profits by way
of bonusses with its c.60,000 workforce, targeting an average bonus payout
of the equivalent of 4 to 6 weeks pay.

*Our people-first approach has guided our company since it was founded and
it means when our company does well, our people do really, really well. Our
people work incredibly hard and deserve to share in Southwest's success.*

An alternative approach: Pizza!

Leading behavioural economics Professor Dan Ariely reported the following
research and an experiment that he carried out with US company Wells Fargo:

In the study, a quarter of the employee base in a particular business unit
were paid an extra $30, another quarter were given a $30 pizza voucher, a third
quarter were sent an encouraging text message from their boss *("well done on
your recent work")* and a control group were given nothing.

The outcome was surprising. Cash worked well on the day, but it had no
lasting benefit. A week later, the group who had received the cash had only the
same levels of motivation and commitment scores that they'd had beforehand.
Pizza fared better! Employee motivation scores stayed higher reflecting the
time till the voucher was redeemed, and often it was being used to help pay
for a meal with friends or family. Even more impactful though was the verbal
"reward". The personal acknowledgement and recognition had the most
enduring and longest lasting benefit. *"The notion that other people respect what you
do sticks with you much longer"*

Professor Ariely has been a leading advocate of employee well-being as the
key to a company's success and has consistently encouraged organisations to
carry out eNPS type research, invest more significantly in employee welfare
and report on this to shareholders.

He cites as a best practice example the global Analytics software company
SAS. They have consistently been recognised as a "best place to work" and the
company describes its business strategy as: "building long term relationships
with our customers, *and* with our employees". The SAS team have developed a
raft of both short term and long term policies, incentives and measures to show
that it cares. They have put especial emphasis on health care for the employee
and all their family, mental health support, funding for employees with short

term cash flow needs, a team of councillors who are responsible for monitoring groups of employees and who have the job to check and report on employee well-being and levels of motivation.

For Professor Ariely, SAS are a best practice example. They join the ranks of LV, Nationwide, Southwest Airlines and other top-performing companies showcased in this book as companies who are getting the Technology:People balance and who seem destined to continue to be future winners.

Chapter 9

How to manage "quiet quitting" – seven rules

A recent Gallup research poll has suggested that "at least 50% of the US workforce consists of quiet quitters: large numbers of employees it seems are just doing the minimum to get by, putting in no more time, effort or enthusiasm than absolutely necessary". And Gallup confirmed this appears to be a growing trend: "people feeling disengaged, not connected to the mission and purpose of the company, and with no motivation or incentive in their current job to go the extra mile."

Of course, the power and value of getting it right with everyone in an organisation, of building great employee engagement is well-documented. There are countless studies showing that it is often the key challenge that every company has to face up to if they are to truly and sustainably succeed. But this now seems to be ever more critical, with hybrid working /WFH (work from home) an accelerating force. In my recruitment work for example, I have placed candidates who even now, 12 to 18 months after joining have perhaps only met their co-workers on a handful of occasions, who have only met their boss a few times, have no real sense of the company culture, not had the chance to make any friends, no "water cooler"/ "coffee in the office kitchen" shared moments and gossip. Hardly surprising perhaps that they struggle to connect, to feel valued and wanted as an important part of the organisation, to feel committed *and inspired*.

So, how can companies breakthrough, how establish that key and essential and heartfelt engagement? How build those great eNPS scores, how ensure that in the next BCG survey that the *Heart* of the company is truly beating well?

In my research and working with companies big and small around the world, I have found there are 7 rules for success, 7 keys to managing "quiet quitting" and transform that into, let's call it: "noisy participation"!

Rule 1: Measure and monitor

We have just read in the previous chapter about eNPS scores. This can be an excellent tool but it does require an HR team to proactively set up a formal employee survey, collect and analyse the data and then produce the report and benchmarks. And that's ok, it is what HR teams have been doing for many years of course. But, there are now a number of new automated Ai-based tools out there. Tools which enable real-time and anonymised data collection on an automated basis and so can give a snapshot at any time, all the time on how employees in your team are feeling, how they are reacting to a new announcement or to rumours about redundancy or to possible decisions to relocate or require people to be in the office 4 or 5 days a week.

Jotform is the leading global app for this, "a gateway for gathering information to propel your business." It has standard template forms that cover a range of HR issues and especially around employee feedback. It's used by the likes of Adobe, Red Bull, Ford and also many smaller businesses and the cost can be as low as £30/month.

Culture Monkey is another increasingly popular tool. They talk about: "Our solutions are all about finding the right employee feedback solution that can help you listen to the honest feedback of your employees and how it can help improve company culture, providing real-time feedback and actionable insights." Their platform is "Ai/GPT powered" to provide HR teams with top feedback themes from employees at a glance, enabling quick identification of any issues and capturing and benchmarking employee sentiment scores.

Engagedly.com is another leading solution that offers real time automated employee feedback. It can also capture verbatim comments and testimonies and distil that into scores and again highlight key issues.

So for any organisation, it is now increasingly easy to monitor and measure by team, by department, by country just how well the workforce is doing. And by looking at the results on an on-going basis, spikes in sentiment, positive or negative, concerns as well as celebrations can all be checked and responded to.

Rule 2: Appoint a Chief Heart Officer

We've previously been reading about Claude Silver as the *Chief Heart Officer* at Vayner Media (a global $150m revenue creative agency). "I work for 800 human beings, 800 souls. I aim to be in touch with the heartbeat of every single person in the company. My role is to infuse the business with empathy and purpose. We want this company to be a place where people *can* find a home. Now more than ever is a time to provide a connecting and emotional landscape where our people can feel realistic and optimistic."

This is such a critical role. It can be buried in an HR team and responsibility diffused across many people but to have a senior go-to champion can make a big impact. I am surprised more companies have not followed the Vayner Media lead. It's as much as anything the symbolism, the flag, the recognition that says that in today's world, we care. We appreciate that people do need that kindness and extra care and support and so setting up, at C-level, a person/a team with the dedicated time and resource to do just that.

The US-based Center for Agile Leadership has also commented on this: "there's no doubt that people leadership and management has become ever more challenging and demanding. But low morale, problems in the workplace, difficulties in a particular team, good bosses as well as bad bosses, all this can be and should be identified almost the moment the issue or opportunity arises. Companies do need to appoint a dedicated champion and process for measuring and monitoring this. Still today in our research, we find that organisations that are posting eg low eNPS scores, low ratings on Glassdoor but we don't then find a coherent or compelling plan to deal with it."

Rule 3: Pay and benefits

Paying competitively ought to be the goal surely of every company. Organisations I have recruited for who aim to benchmark and pay towards the top quartile, such as Aviva, LEGO, Unilever, do tend to attract and get the best people, as would be expected. But it surprises me how many companies will proudly tell me our policy is deliberately *not* to pay top quartile, "we want people to join us because of who we are, not because of the money."

That noble philosophy may sound good and idealistic and may indeed be appropriate in the not-for-profit sector where individuals are highly motivated to perhaps support a particular cause. But in the private /commercial sector?

Research by Willis Towers Watson has shown that 47% of people left their jobs because they could get more money elsewhere and that 39% of people felt that there was no point going the extra mile because they did not feel they were being paid their market rate. Of course, people will always look for higher pay & benefits, but surely no reason to add fuel to that fire by deliberately paying low quartile?

Rule 4: Career path

Nearly half (47%) of employees say that they don't see a clear path to progression in their current job. This is according to new research conducted by IRIS Software Group (IRIS), in partnership with YouGov. The IRIS research showed there is sometimes a lack of transparency between managers and their teams over career goals and that often current HR tools and systems are not built to best manage and support employee progression. "Workers today want purpose and meaning from their work and a clear timeline of what's next for them in the workplace – and rightly so."

Professional Services firms are the stand-out success stories however in this regard. Law firms, Accountants and the major Banks all set out clear plans and timelines for promotion. So for example at the top 4 Accountancy firms, EY, KPMG, Deloitte and PWC, a graduate on joining knows exactly what they need to achieve and by when to get to the next pay and promotion level, from Junior Associate to Snr Associate to Manager, Snr Mgr, Director, Managing Director to Partner. "Here at PWC, you can expect a clear and structured career path through the levels from internship to partnership".

There's another good stand-out example from AT&T. They have a mantra: "every employee should be the CEO of their own career". Each and every AT&T employee has a personal careers dashboard. It shows all the development milestones they need to hit to get to the next level in the organisation. It's tailored and adapted for each person. It reflects appraisal and 360 feedback as well personal performance. "Our Future Ready program is transparent. It shows what competencies people need to reach to achieve a particular goal and sets out all the training that will be provided to enable that person to get there".

Rule 5: Bonuses/incentives

We have spoken about Nationwide and LV. They are respected leaders in the field of employee engagement. And in the context of pay and benefits, it's probably fair to say that their base pay structure is mid-tier and not upper quartile. Yet people want to work at those companies. The pay is fair and reasonable but most importantly, they are great places to work. Employees talk with an enthusiasm and passion about working at these companies and word gets round about how positive is the culture and employee experience.

The sort of testimonies these two companies get make them clear stand-outs:

"great culture and ethic of care for customers"
"flexibility and good work life balance"
"some really great people at the office and at the branch"
"they seem to really care about how we are"
"all our team are saying we would recommend working here".

And for example worth recapping just how well LV does look after its people:

> *There's a generous array of employee benefits to help their staff engage.*
>
> *Everyone is eligible for the LV bonus scheme, all are able to participate in the pension plan up to a 14% matched contribution, there are coffee cards for new joiners, healthcare, holidays for top-performing employees and their families, weekly thank you cards and gift vouchers with more than 23,000 sent out in the last year (workforce of 5000), flexible working, crowdsourcing /funding plans for new ideas, a customer leadership academy…a lot of effort going in to make employees feel valued and motivated.*

At Nationwide:

> *We feel that bonuses don't need to be confined to a once a year reward payable 15 months after the start of the year. They can be paid to have an immediate impact, now, recognising and rewarding today."*
>
> *So, for all, vouchers /employee rewards **each week** for work well-done, celebrations of employees "who go the extra mile" with their stories published weekly for all to read, long service awards…employees feel valued and their efforts recognised.*

Rule 6: Train the managers!

If the new paradigm includes remote working, hybrid workforces, distributed employees, located potentially all over the world, how can managers best manage, how ensure the right levels of employee motivation and engagement, how ensure low to zero levels of "quiet quitting"?

Most have not been trained in this new world of work, in many instances they will have themselves grown up in a more traditional environment where employees came to the office 5 days/week and it was often relatively easier to identify who was committed and who was disaffected.

AXA, Cromwell Group, Siemens, Virgin Money are all examples of organisations who have recognised this "new paradigm" and have been proactive in dealing with it.

For example at AXA, they have launched a programme called "Smart Working". *Each* team has got together and been asked to all *co-design* a team agreement about working arrangements, how much time in the office and when, agreed days in the week when they all need to be there, socials booked in the calendar, commitments eg to 2 hour response to calendar invites, 1 hour response to calls, setting-up mentor and coaching times, an acceptance that hybrid working has its advantages, but also its disadvantages and an open dialogue about how each person on the team expects to respond.

Each manager was also invited to join the "Smart Ready" training programs, a mix of virtual and in-person courses which focussed on communication and engagement styles, how to encourage and most importantly celebrate good performance and also how to identify if an employee is struggling and how to help them.

> *Retaining key talent is one of the biggest issues. It's putting the brakes on growth. It's become more challenging in the new hybrid world of work. Businesses must leave no stone unturned to develop new solutions to manage in the best possible way in this new climate.*
> – Matthew Fell, as CBI Chief UK Policy Director

Rule 7: Attractive workspace

Is the office attractive, is it a nice place to come to work, is it easy to get to eg within range of public transport options, is there somewhere to park my car? Is it modern, does it have good aircon for the summer days, are there coffee shops nearby, do people rate it as a good environment to work in?

If an organisation wants to engage and incentivise and motivate then surely there's an increasing premium on providing the most positive work place experience. The bar has been raised by the emergence of new flexible office spaces. Often located in city centres with modern facilities, attractive design and typically with a good buzzy atmosphere. Such workspaces have reset expectations about what an office can look and feel like.

Knight Frank, the property experts, have said they are seeing a "flight to quality for premium office space." As leases come to an end, companies are often looking for "up to 20% or 30% less space" but in an area and style which can provide more. Meantime, "Grade B space is seeing a significant increase in vacancy rates".

Research by Microsoft found that 38% of employees felt their office "was not an attractive place to come to work" and that can provide a further disconnect between the company and the employee. Getting the office workspace right is not by itself of course going to be an answer but it can be an integral part of this "7 rules" plan.

★ ★ ★

Employee engagement is not quick and easy to accomplish. It requires the whole leadership of the company to make it a core and critical priority. Even better if those senior managers are trained and also measured on staff engagement in their team, and benchmarked versus others.

Retaining staff, building commitment and excitement, creating an environment where people want to and regularly do go the extra mile, where that mode of behaviour becomes the norm and the standard, that will always be an ongoing challenge and opportunity. Smaller companies and ventures can find it easier where there is a shared and common purpose, where there can be more intimacy and esprit de corps. Larger organisations by definition will find that harder, and harder still to enshrine that motivation organisation-wide and not just in a few teams in a few areas.

We've all seen and sometimes had the privilege of working in well-run, well-managed, inspiring work places. We can point to that manager or that person who was "just brilliant" at getting the best out of everyone. The challenge now is just that bit harder in this new world of work and so we do have to learn to adapt how we manage, how we build teams and how best motivate, sustainably and successfully.

"The way to get started is to quit talking and begin doing."
– Walt Disney

"The best time to plant a tree was 20 years ago. The second best time is now."
– Aristotle

"Good teams create the building blocks for success"
– Dwight Eisenhower

Chapter 10

Building an effective data, AI and analytics team and capability

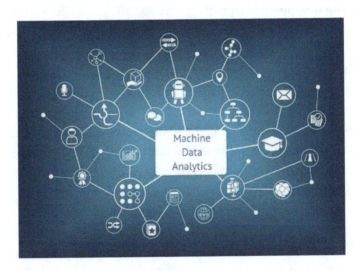

A recent KPMG survey described Data, Ai & Analytics expertise as: "the most in-demand skill sets" with 49% of companies saying they struggled to find the right talent to lead this area. The Harvard Business Review has declared that "data science and analytics are the sexiest jobs of the century!" Research company Gartner has suggested that there will be as many as 4 million new data and analytics jobs coming up worldwide over the next few years. And for example, the US Bureau of Labor Statistics recorded more than 170,000 open jobs in the Data arena at the time of writing.

Getting insight out of data, driving ideas and innovation that can better target and engage customers, enabling more informed decision-making, helping manage and reduce risk, improving performance, taking advantage of machine learning tools…all these applications of data management, analytics and insight are key areas of opportunity of course in today's data rich world.

But in a recent survey by BARC Research, only 26% of execs interviewed felt that their companies were making effective use of the data they had. That's a significant majority who felt that data was not being fully exploited in their organisation. As a sign of what's missing, or perhaps better said, what the potential could be, 54% of execs in the same survey said that they did hope! to get more involved in using data insights in the future.

There's a massive untapped potential here. Everyone will agree about the "power of data". But it's often the exploitation of that data that is still missing.

The focus on the power of data and analytics has been increased of course because of developments in data science. Machine Learning and Artificial Intelligence are bringing a whole new wave of ideation and insight and new ways of working and new possible streams of revenue and profitability. It's a massive opportunity and companies have raced to build their data science teams. This is especially true for example in financial services where companies like Aviva, Barclays, Zurich Insurance and others now often talk about having teams of more than 500 to 1000 data scientists across their international businesses all focussed on next generation opportunities.

This rush to data science has had several consequences. Demand exceeds supply. There just aren't enough data scientists to go round. It means that salaries have increased significantly as companies find they are forced to pay a premium. And it's not uncommon to hear that a Bank or Insurer is in the market with a recruitment goal of hiring eg 25 data scientists in the next 3 months - for just one of their local country operating teams. So even new graduates out of university are finding they are being swept up in this enthusiastic rush. And they are attracted to it as the salaries on offer are high. It also means that many such data teams are relatively junior, maybe only a few years work experience and so lack leaders with deep managerial experience. They may all be good computer scientists and software engineers but their stakeholder management skills, their political nous on how best to operate inside a large corporation, their interpersonal skills and ways of communicating...these sort of necessary team leadership skills are sometimes lacking.

All this has led to a disconnect between Senior Exec / Board level ambitions and expectations versus what is actually happening in the data science team, their output and what they are delivering. The data geeks are busy developing new AI tools and algorithms but all that isn't necessarily translating into new product / service features and solutions that do make an impact in the market *and* deliver the RoI.

So a number of organisations are now adding further to their data science investments by inserting Transformation experts who can review the way data science is organised and "operationalise and systematise" the way it works, its processes and core interactions so that the substantial potential can be captured and realised. Though there's a need to drive this carefully as too much control can of course extinguish the necessary spirit of innovation and entrepreneurship that can uncover the big new idea that can make the difference.

Companies are learning. They have rushed to hire the people and now need to find the best ways to make that investment pay back. Making it work may need the insertion of "transformation experts" but it might also be about establishing a more effective structure which encourages the broader company-wide adoption of the data science ideas and capabilities.

In many organisations for example, we find the data/analytics team set up in an individual business area, operating in silos with their own agendas and reporting lines and so will often only collaborate cross-function /across the company to share ideas if there is a clear mandate and shared view that this is indeed a strategic priority.

Typically data science sits in the IT /Technology group. Historically it is this function who have been the early initiators of projects around data and data warehousing. They have the relationships with the analytical software vendors like S&P or Adobe or SAS or Acquia/AgilOne or the many smaller alternative suppliers and so will likely be the early advocates and adopters. But as a recent Accenture Interactive survey pointed out: "CIO leadership of data and analytics can work well. But that is provided it is *intertwined* with the other c-Suite leaders and especially the CMO and the customer marketing team. Without very close collaboration, data and analytics can end up being an IT team software project instead of an insight into performance and the voice of the customer".

Recent research from an IBM /Constellation ThinkTank has also highlighted that collaboration around the data science agenda is going to be a key and that a failure to collaborate is a major reason for lack of progress. They advocate that more CMOs and more Marketing departments do now need to step forward. And if not seize control of this area at least make sure that the "intertwining" is happening and working. The research suggests that Marketers are not intuitively comfortable with data and detailed analysis. But with the proliferation of marketing and communication channels, IBM /Constellation emphasise it is imperative for Marketing teams to still be the "voice of the customer" and so have that close insight and understanding to better drive performance insight and more personalised and more cost-effective customer activity.

The challenge then is how to build an effective data and data science team that works, that does effectively cut through the data value chain and deliver the RoI all are expecting. If we look at the skills and jobs required to build this capability then it's clear we are looking at a substantial task of team development and cross-company integration.

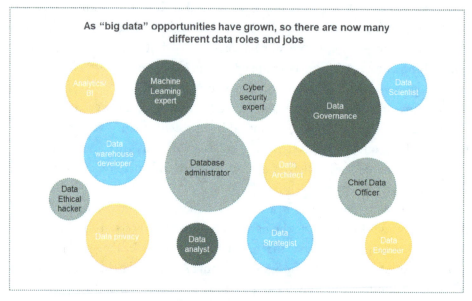

This shows just how many different and specific skills and areas of expertise are required. Companies may often ask to hire eg a "Head of AI" or a Chief Data Officer but when asked what they want that person to do and focus on, then the answer is sometimes vague and indeterminate. Yet, clearly any "Head of Data" will need to have a clear remit and set of deliverables to do their job properly and making sure they have the right background and specific skills is critical. For example, for a Head of Ai role, do we want a software engineer, a data geek or are their interpersonal and team leadership skills more essential given the state of the team's development? Depending on the answer will clearly influence the sort of CV the "Head of" person should have.

Assuming there are budgets and scope to build out an effective Data team, then the suggested start-point is to hire in the **Data Strategist**. This person is the one who will build the business case, meet the key stakeholders, identify the potential "size of prize", determine at a top line a possible team and possible investment and so define the possible outcomes and RoI. The person best placed to do that may not even have any data expertise themselves. But they bring an MBA-type, commercial approach, can take a fresh perspective and critically can interact at Board level to determine a strategic plan of action.

Once agreed then there will be a number of key next step appointments needed:

1. The Data Architect

This person will be the designer, they will develop the technical architecture that needs to be developed. They will decide for example on what software platform(s), whether to build in-house or use established software tools and solutions, how much can /should be Cloud-based, who best to partner with.

In many ways this is the most critical hire and appointment as this person is determining the whole future roadmap and blueprint for the organisation. So finding someone who has "been there and done it" and done it successfully is so important.

They also need to have enough credibility and authority that they can win the respect and support especially of the CTO but also the other key business leaders who can accept being guided by this person.

2. Data Analysts

This may be a small team and they are the ones who will feed off the work from the Strategist and the Architect. They will be getting into the detail, understanding the use-case requirements, investigating the areas of opportunity so they can spec out exactly what level of software and functionality and skills are needed.

3. Data Engineers

These are the people who will build-out the overall architecture and design. They may have expertise in enterprise data solutions such as Oracle, IBM or Microsoft or more dedicated niche providers such as Tibco, Precisely/EnterWorks or RiverSand. They will be building the infrastructure that will enable the data management. They will also be the integrators who will ensure the interoperability of any new solutions with the main operating platform. They will also have responsibility for delivery, testing and maintenance.

4. Data Scientists

The data scientists will be the machine learning/AI experts. They may have PhDs in Maths or Statistics or Computer Sciences. They are excited about building new products /services and applications. They have been described as "the alchemists of the 21st century"! Their core skill is turning raw data into insight and they will want to be hands-on coders as that is what most energises them.

This also highlights the earlier point that as this area scales up so inevitably it will need team leaders and managers who will need to spend more time managing and communicating while perhaps coaching the more junior developers and this interpersonal skill set is in very short supply in this data science arena. Not easy to find PhD data scientists who can interact confidently and effectively with senior Business /Function heads across the organisation and translate the Tech talk into commercial terms which others can understand!

5. Data Governance

In today's world, data management, data privacy, who has access, how data can be used, what processes need to be in place to ensure data is managed.. this area needs to be taken care of. And in the Financial Services sector especially there are substantial amounts of regulation and compliance that need to be implemented, monitored and reported on. It is a significant and now high-profile role. It may well be a job taken by a former practising lawyer who has that attention to minute detail and protocol and can manage through the substantial layers of bureaucracy.

6. The CSO

The Chief Security Officer is possibly the least attractive job! This is the person who will get the call at 2am on a Sunday morning if there has been a leak of personal data. This is the person who is most in the spotlight unfortunately if something goes wrong! So those who take the role will likely be obsessive security experts who will be trying to ensure that nothing can go wrong. They will likely employ their own 24/7 "ethical hacking" teams who are constantly testing the systems' defences and identifying any potential leak or lack of adequate security before an outside third party can discover it.

A report from Cisco /IT Governance shows there are more and more major targeted cyber-attacks potentially impacting millions of personal data records each time. In addition, research shows that at least a third of companies have experienced some form of hacking. Companies like Uber, Equifax and Under Armour have reported attacks eg affecting, in the case of Equifax, more than 150 million people. And the costs of managing and defending keep going up. Aside from the team needed to manage these situations, companies say that costs have increased by more than 20% and now there are ransom-ware costs, loss of information, potential loss of customers, the adverse publicity…it's estimated that the cost to Equifax was more than \$4bn.

The biggest area of potential damage is through email. Simple phishing which encourages an email to be opened, a link clicked can cause untold damage and some 90% of all data breaches come about this way. This is something that companies can try to protect against and one example comes from Nationwide, the UK Bank /Building Society. They have trained all their 18,000 employees in cyber security and have set up a very rigorous system around that. Test emails are periodically sent out to staff to check if they have understood all the training. If an employee nevertheless does click the test link, then they are asked to go to be retrained. If the same person makes the mistake a second time then they are given a formal warning. And a third time has the risk of being asked to leave the company.

This may sound like a tough regime, but it is inevitably the way most companies are headed and will have to set up some sort of similar monitoring programme to heighten awareness around this issue.

That's why the CSO job is probably one of the least popular and at the same time the most onerous!

★ ★ ★

If all this data team is to work effectively it will naturally need the right leadership and there are three key roles that should be considered:

1. Chief Data Officer
2. Director of Data Science
3. Director of Customer Insight & Analytics

1. Chief Data Officer

Forrester research summed up this crucial leadership role:

> *The CDO is the senior executive who bears the overall responsibility for the firm's enterprise-wide data and information strategy, governance, control, policy development and effective exploitation. The CDO's role will combine accountability and responsibility for information protection and privacy, information governance, data quality and data life cycle management, along with the exploitation of data assets to create business value.*

Gartner predicts that every regulated corporation will have to have a formal CDO or equivalent and that 90% + of all Fortune 1000 companies will also have such a dedicated leadership role.

The CDO role is wide, it sits across the whole data value chain:

The Data Value Chain

The skills background of a CDO will likely include:

- steeped in data world
- perhaps with a Business Intelligence /Analytics expertise
- though not necessarily a "techie"
- someone with strategic nous, great stakeholder management skills and commercial flair;
  - eg 1 recent CDO appointment had 25 yrs experience, had been at data consultancy Dunnhumby for 15yrs, and role there had been as MD /Commercial /Country Mgr, so very immersed in the data world but with strong commercial and c-suite skills
  - eg another recent CDO appointment had a PhD in Statistics, had moved from statistician into data analysis /data science and then taking broader responsibilities with more senior data management responsibilities
  - a third such example is a CDO with a very strong Computer Science background who was previously the CIO at the same company so knew the company, culture and key people and how to navigate the matrix and politics to get things done!

2. Director of Data Science

AstraZeneca have described their Director of Data Science in this way:

Lead, promote, investigate, develop and implement novel statistical, data mining, machine learning, Ai approaches and solutions, skills, capabilities, tools, processes and standard methodologies.

Like many companies they have set up a Data Lab, in their organisation called "The Advanced Analytics Centre" which is their hub of data science experts, integrating historical data compiled from multiple data sources, with local insights from the Marketing teams, to inform new product design and refine trial and execution. The Centre uses advanced predictive techniques and "real-time in-depth multivariate statistical metrics and visualizations for in-flight clinical trial monitoring."

The skills background will need to include:

- excellent understanding of machine learning techniques and algorithms such as kNN, Naïve Bayes, SVM, Decision Forest, VertexAi, Nvidia Instant NeRF etc
- experience with common data science tool kits such as R, Weka, Python /NumPy, MatLab etc
- expertise with OpenAI/GPT
- experience with data visualisation tools such as D3.js, GGplot2 etc
- proficiency in using query languages such as SQL, Hive, Pig etc
- understanding of NoSQL databases such as MongoDB, Cassandra and Hbase
- strong statistical skills
- Agile /Scrum/proto-type mind-set /methodology
- potentially also taking in "big data" responsibilities across the whole organisation, eg building a "big data" interrogation environment with eg Hadoop, RapidMiner software skills
- software engineering background
- highly analytical
- someone who enjoys data and detail and the software to understand it!

3. Director of Customer Insight & Analytics

Under Armour describe their Head of Customer Insight & Analytics in this way:

Determine the shape of UA's future including target markets, product development, marketing investments and marketing messaging.

This individual is the link to the product, brand and category teams who are charged with creating breakthrough product and messaging that engages the needs of our customers. This person is charged to bring the customer profiles, personalities and needs to life within the Company and to the broader organization of category and regional country leads.

Equal part anthropologist, futurist, moderator, influencer and analyst, this senior contributor will be instrumental to driving the intersection of consumer needs to cultural relevance across new wearable technologies, connected fitness, performance wear categories and design style.

A significant part of the work is to guide the sales and marketing teams, to identify most promising leads and customer segments, to evaluate the different parts of the marketing mix and spend and to optimise that spend to maximise the return.

The person is also responsible for linking the consumer to all of the key phases of the innovation lifecycle. The work will span deep qualitative and quantitative immersion, multi-source ideation, trend research and rigorous analytics. The knowledge base / toolkit required of this individual will reflect that diversity of insight needs."

This sort of job description for this role is typically wide-ranging and optimistic! It lands substantial responsibility for growth and innovation onto one core team; provide the analytic-based insight to drive improved customer and consumer engagement and conversion. It does naturally therefore require not just the analytical skills but also outstanding stakeholder manager skills to get the insights that come through adopted, implemented and embraced!

★ ★ ★

There's a strong business case for investing in this whole area. According to research from Capgemini:

- 59% of companies who champion the use of customer analytics are likely to have profit well above their competitors.
- Such companies are 6.5 times more likely to retain customers, 7.4 times more likely to outperform their competitors on making sales to existing customers (upsell and cross sell strategies), and nearly 19 times more likely to achieve above-average profitability.
- The four key areas where integrating customer analytics across the value chain of a business are paying off: enabling integrated multichannel marketing (29%), frontline embedding of analytics (28%), expanding customer analytics across the value chain (27%), and processing real-time data (24%).

Recent appointments in this area will typically see people with many years' experience in analytics, but importantly this will be *customer* analytics and not say pricing risk or fraud analytics which tend to attract people eg with an Actuarial interest and background. What works best here are those who are also would-be marketers and want to get close to consumers and customers and so would be comfortable reporting into the Chief Marketing Officer or the Chief Data Officer or as in some companies, both!

★ ★ ★

How do all these roles come together, what sort of Data structure and department should be established which can capture all these core skills and business needs and requirements?

Large scale data teams are still relatively new and have often grown up through a series of independent, not joined-up initiatives with eg both Marketing and IT building their own analytics /data science capability or in the context of a multi-national, each business unit or country market developing their own teams using their local data and each in doing so choosing their own data and analytics platforms, their own governance rules, their own approaches to eg data privacy, instead of there being a joined-up group wide strategy and plan that can capture best practices and synergy and make data work seamlessly across all parts of the organisation.

The org structure here looks at a potential recommended Data function led by the CDO:

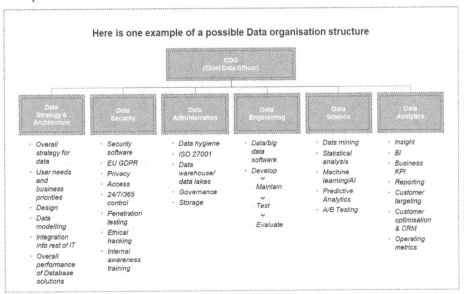

Here is one example of a possible Data organisation structure

Data Strategy & Architecture	Data Security	Data Administration	Data Engineering	Data Science	Data Analytics
· Overall strategy for data · User needs and business priorities · Design · Data modelling · Integration into rest of IT · Overall performance of Database solutions	· Security software · EU GDPR · Privacy · Access · 24/7/365 control · Penetration testing · Ethical hacking · Internal awareness training	· Data hygiene · ISO 27001 · Data warehouse/ data lakes · Governance · Storage	· Data/big data software · Develop ᵛ Maintain ᵛ Test ᵛ Evaluate	· Data mining · Statistical analysis · Machine learning/AI · Predictive Analytics · A/B Testing	· Insight · BI · Business KPI · Reporting · Customer targeting · Customer optimisation & CRM · Operating metrics

It does embrace all the key skills and components discussed here. It does assume that an organisation will have the budgets and scale to fund the team and resources described. But it is critical to understand that for a Chief Data Officer to do their job, to deliver to expectations, to manage and protect and exploit as the job specs describe, then the CDO does need this sort of team, it does need these skills and these aspects looked after by people with the right experience. And if there were to be compromise then what leave out? Cyber Security? That would be almost negligent. Customer Analytics? That could miss significant new customer revenue opportunities. Each part of the structure is key, and any organisation of size is urged to build as much of this as is affordable and possible.

In terms of reporting lines, research from Gartner and Information Week show that there are many different options and variations:

The race is on to recruit the best of the talent available in the marketplace. Market feedback shows that good data people are getting recruiter/headhunter calls every week! So for a company to attract the best talent they must be able to demonstrate a genuine commitment to this area, a readiness to invest and have thought through reporting lines and stakeholder interests so they can convince a new recruit that a data leadership role with them can truly make a difference and can succeed. That will be a critical underpinning to turn data into a true driver of RoI and success.

Chapter 11

The still untapped potential of effective customer data and analytics

We've talked about building the Data, Ai & Analytics team, the key roles and responsibilities, the core skills and expertise required in each quite different role, we've looked at how to structure the team and who it should report to, so let's now look at how that team can indeed deliver and focus especially on customer analytics and the potential to unlock new sources of revenue growth and customer engagement.

A few recent headlines show the prominence and priority that many organisations are giving to this D&A space.

Here at Coca-Cola, we are expecting a high impact with our consumers and retail customers from Generative Ai over the next 3 years.

GSK (Glaxo) announce partnership with McLaren Formula 1 motor racing to access their expertise in big data analytics.

Bayer, ABB Electronics, B2B pioneers unlock the value of real-time customer analytics.

IBM now have a team of 20,000 worldwide focussed on Advanced Analytics and Ai.

American Express finds new revenue growth through deep analysis and research.

Uber, Amazon, Netflix have been leaders in customer-focused data science, machine learning and predictive analytics, but they are joined by a host of others.

Alexander Stojanovic, former VP at eBay, describes how analytics is at the heart of their key business decision-making:

If we truly understand the customer data, understand the journey from beginning to end, then we have the strategic horsepower to influence the entire organisation.

★ ★ ★

Few doubt the value of analysis and insight to drive better decision-making. In these days where there is a "deluge of available data" and an ever-growing array of tools and solutions becoming available, there is an imperative now to find ways to exploit this opportunity, to capture, interrogate and find the key insights that can drive competitive advantage.

However, a recent study from the Aberdeen Group showed that a surprising 78%! of company executives felt that their organisations "struggled to make effective use of customer data". At the same time, those who were able to master customer analysis and insight showed remarkable results. They could point to increases in:

- net new customer revenues
- revenues from customer referrals
- cross-sell and upsell gains
- plus improvements in annual % customer service costs.

For the winners, the "customer data masters", success is not only the preserve of large multi-nationals; smaller local companies can also take advantage without spending $Ms to do so. Here's a few case study examples:

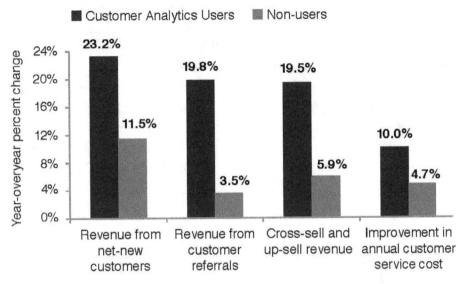

Customer Analytics Users Maximise their Revenue

■ Customer Analytics Users   ■ Non-users

Adidas

Lia Vakoutis, when Senior Director at Adidas, described how they mined social media data to drive new product sales:

We used to prepare promotions months in advance. Because of the cost and time invested we used to just roll them out hoping they'd work ok. But if they didn't it was too late to do much to change. So we made a decision to move from "reactive marketing" to "predictive marketing".

To achieve this shift in Marketing and promotions planning, we now use a variety of tools to monitor social media sentiment including SalesForce Social Studio/Statusbrew (social media /Marcomms monitoring in real time), Meltwater (provider of infographics and reports on competitive social media performance), Brandwatch (manages /analyses big data). All these can work together to produce the most detailed picture of what's going on in our social media world.

Adidas focus on the 5 key social media fora: Twitter/X, YouTube, TikTok, Facebook and Instagram. They are analysing for example some

1200 sports and soccer specific message boards, blogs, news sites. A recent campaign count showed they had analysed over 4 million pieces of information across 17 markets in multiple languages. Because the analysis and insights are coming through in real time, Adidas can shift promotions, feature the sports stars who are getting more traction and response, change promotional material, add or change copy, influence conversations and also react immediately to competitor activity. "It's just a brilliant way to test what works and what does not, and be able to react instantaneously. In one recent campaign we were able to test and monitor 300 different concepts in one 48 hour period".

Amazon.com

Amazon are so often cited these days as best practice, but when I interviewed them, they spoke about the following:

*Of all the things we do today, we believe it's our **real time customer analytics that make the difference**.*

We have a team monitoring customer activity by the second and we can see immediately what's working, what's not, we can identify price change opportunities, page lay-out changes, product-bundling and we can check this across all users and our whole customer base.

What really makes this data monitoring work is that we use it and make the changes in real time too. How do we do that? We have a "virtual circle" of Analytics, UX/Conversion and Web Dev. That is made up of three core groups of people who work very actively together. They are co-located, they report to one person, they are the key commercial grouping.

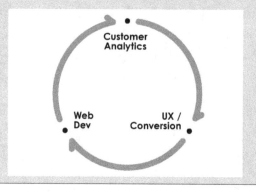

That sort of real-time analytical *plus* change capability is rare. Some companies with similar fast-moving /fashion /consumer-driven businesses do try to organise in this way. For example retailers John Lewis and Next. But what even these successful organisations lack is that corresponding real-time change capability. They still impose too many checks and controls to make that work easily.

One more case study comparing *Starbucks* with *Pret a Manger*.

Starbucks introduced its customer loyalty scheme some 20 yrs ago. It is recognised as being one of the most successful loyalty programs. The My Starbucks rewards program started as a simple payment card before it gradually evolved into the successful rewards scheme it is today ("one sip gets you gold status").

Howard Schultz, when CEO and then Chairman, updated shareholders at an AGM:

> *More than half of My Starbucks's /Rewards 31 million members are high-spending gold members, in addition more than 23 million use the mobile-payments app and in one quarter alone more than $4bn was loaded by members onto their cards.*
>
> *We can do all this and make it easy for members because we have invested in building our customer database and capability. It means that we can see what our members are doing and critically these days we can personalise and tailor all our customer communications so each member can feel some personal connection with us.*

Starbucks uses Oracle customer relationship management (CRM) software as its loyalty system, which is tied to the Oracle ERP platform. This delivers a combination of transactional, analytical and engagement features to manage all the sources of customer data, no matter if it's in-store or on mobile.

Starbucks has massive amounts of data that needs continuous cleansing and analysis and with c. 4 billion+ cups of coffee sold each year that is a lot of data! "…and we still have not been able to get all the insights out that are possible".

Pret a Manger on the other hand in its early days took a very different approach to customer loyalty. Instead of building extensive customer databases, their approach was to leave loyalty up to each employee's discretion.

The concept was to encourage store staff to get to know their customers and work to build up local support through that more personal recognition and reward. And for many years that worked very well: "we had looked at loyalty cards but in our early days we did not want to spend all that money building up some large scale Clubcard-style database". Instead, the Pret approach was described as "freestyle and fun" empowering employees to give away eg free coffees.

As Pret has got larger, it now has 600 outlets across 15 countries, so it increasingly felt the need to find more sophisticated and systematised ways to get to know its customers, to stay in touch with them and incentivise them to keep coming back. So it has now taken the Starbucks approach with the launch of its Pret Perks App which rewards with eg a free coffee after every 10 purchases and perhaps most importantly provides the customer data, which Pret can now try to mine, gain insights, build loyalty and monetise.

With these sort of case studies showing what possible and what can be achieved, why is that 78% of executives in the Aberdeen Group research are frustrated with their own company's lack of progress in this area?

A recent Harvard Business Review study showed that 53% of execs surveyed by them felt that: "getting the customer experience right" was an important strategic priority (one wonders about the other 47% who did not agree with that statement!). But there was a broad consensus about the key challenges to be overcome:

(i)   *Proving the RoI*: companies find that while there can be many customer improvement initiatives it can be difficult to clearly attribute and show which initiative is delivering what RoI and this makes further investment cases hard to validate. So half of the companies in the HBR survey said that: "it's still a struggle to fund customer experience programs"

(ii)   *"Deluge of data":* "there's now so much potential data available but what are we going to do with it all?"

(iii) *Multi-channel complexity:* "we are looking at data from web, store, email, social media, tele-sales, call centre, field sales, Mobile, customer query handling, past purchase records…even assuming we capture all this data accurately, which we don't, then how do we get to a unified view?"

(iv)   *Data integration /standardisation:* Only 18% of companies in the HBR survey felt that they had an integrated data capture system. "We have different departments operating in silos with their own databases and drawing their own conclusions. Efforts to tie the data together meet 100 reasons why not".

(v)   *Lack of key skills:* Is there a Chief Data Officer? If there is, how much of that person's time is deep in data science, or do they also work to drive the insights into the Marketing and customer decision-making process? Is each of the areas in the Customer value chain effectively being staffed and led? Is that whole chain of value being brought together, coordinated and championed by one senior Data/Analytics /Insight Officer?

(vi)   *No unifying Dashboard /metrics /KPi:* Both in the HBR and the previously mentioned Aberdeen Group surveys, a key reason cited for lack of progress was the absence of a clear set of metrics and KPi. There was no agreed measures of what was successful customer experience, there was no comparison of how well the company was doing vs. competitors in this area or vs. more widely relevant benchmarks, no way of identifying and agreeing what was working and what not, no insight to show what the improvement gaps might be, no understanding of what the full potential could be if customer engagement was truly optimised.

(vii) *No use of NPS:* NPS or Net Promoter Score is fast becoming the global standard for measuring how well a company is delivering on customer service. It's a system pioneered by Bain Consulting and Satmetrix. Its power lies in the monitoring and measuring the NPS trend and benchmarking vs competition.

Those who embrace NPS see it as the key catalyst and start of their Customer Analytics journey. "It's an objective market study, it shows how we're doing and it compares our performance, it has galvanised us into defining what other metrics we needed and how to go about getting that data and insight together".

★ ★ ★

Let's look at two company cases studies where they seem to have effectively managed their way through these significant challenges:

Countax/Ariens are an inspiring manufacturing benchmark, www.countax. co.uk. They produce lawnmowers and other outdoor equipment, a good UK-base, distributing worldwide, just 120 staff. Darren Spencer, one of the former senior Directors, commented: "Our business had long suffered with insufficient or difficult to access data across all aspects of our operation and especially in better understanding our distributor and end-user customer base. Quick access to information we trusted was just not possible. We had the data, we just couldn't use it or it was very painful to get it!"

Countax hired a Business Intelligence software firm called Matillion who set about implementing a SaaS data warehouse solution which would integrate with their ERP as well as with other in-house developed bespoke systems. The areas of BI and data integration covered Sales, Inventory, Supply Chain, Customer Data and customer purchase /contact history. Data inputs and definitions were defined, the key dashboard metrics were agreed and a major effort took place to unify and standardise so there would be a single and common view of all the data insights.

Now Countax has a self-service BI environment which is designed at various levels of detail so that even the non-data literate can access, interpret and digest. "The reporting ability that comes from this business intelligence has greatly helped. We now rely on these analyses to guide the strategic direction; we didn't have this level of visibility before. And because we have a common dashboard it makes our management meetings much quicker and easier, there's no debate about the data, it's now simply about what actions to take...wish we had done this years ago!"

Sainsbury's: as CEO, Simon Roberts spoke about how he sees customer data analytics as the key to the company's future success: "We are aiming for a future where we know every single customer on an intimate basis...we want to be able to predict what our customers will need, when they'll need and how best to deliver that to them".

Sainsbury's has been on a long journey collecting and building "a vault of customer data". But in its early days that information was accessible to only a few analysts and coders. " We weren't using the information to its full capacity, it wasn't easily accessible to Buying, Merchandising and Marketing and so we were short of the customer insights needed to break new ground",

Sainsbury's long ago teamed up with Aimia (and subsequently acquired them!). Aimia are customer analytics/loyalty specialists, and together developed a 6-point strategy and change programme:

(i) *Identify the key metrics*: This was a critical step: what are the key measures of effective customer engagement and how be sure to measure those things that can truly drive sales. Sainsbury's has developed a wide list of these KPi which include basics such as trends in average spend, basket size, frequency of purchase, customer lifetime value etc to derive a "loyalty index" and allies with that with more emotional / sentiment scores derived from research, online surveys, social media and NPS scores. All this done not just at a store level but where possible at an individual customer level.

(ii) *Train staff, continuously, in Customer Service*

(iii) *Build a dedicated team*: now c. 120+ people responsible for customer data management, analysis, reporting and insight. Reports are tailored for each department so eg Buying will get its own set of analyses and insights as well as seeing the bigger picture.

(iv) *Monitor use of the data insights.* A key task of all senior managers is to ensure the data insights are followed through and actioned.

(v) *Personalisation*: Develop customer marketing and promotion campaigns and initiatives that allow individualised, personalised customer comms.

(vi) *Supplier investment*: Sainsbury's has worked with its supplier base to give them access to this customer data and insights. The aim is to help suppliers identify what sells best, innovate and develop products that customers want, see which promotions work best and generally enable them to maximise their own business activities.

In a recent statement, CEO Roberts has re-emphasised the need to continue to invest in this area: "It's on-going to address the changing and multi-channel needs of customers. So we want to still improve the in-store customer experience with further investment in staff training and a new automated system to track availability. We are also committing to further systems infrastructure to create a single view of customers, leading to increasingly effective interactions"

★ ★ ★

Whether it's GSK, IBM, Starbucks, Netflix or Countax, whether B2C or B2B, in today's highly competitive world, companies are of course having to work harder to grow and be successful. Few would argue that "developing an intimate understanding of our customer" is not a major imperative and need. The challenge is to establish that company-wide commitment to getting those data analyses and insights together in a unified form that can drive decision-making and enhanced customer engagement. Will future Aberdeen Group surveys continue to show 78% of companies struggling to build an effective customer analytics platform?

Chapter 12

Winning in the talent wars – the new 1-week paradigm

The next two chapters look at how to find the best talent and how to build the best teams to go after this compelling Tech/Ai/Data agenda and become as best placed as possible to succeed.

Why do the GAFA (Google, Apple, Facebook and Amazon) companies seem to always get the best talent? Is it just because they've got strong Brand names, is it because they pay more or is it something much more straightforward that any company could replicate? Is there a "secret to their success" that other companies can learn from and embrace?

This chapter sets out the answer and it all comes down to the new paradigm in the talent wars game. It's about using Agile methods to win. Managing a recruiting process that is done simultaneously, not in waterfall. Prioritising, galvanising team, setting short time lines, having clear goals -day by day (not month by month): establishing a new *1-week paradigm.*

It's the idea of moving very fast once top talent is identified. It's about building a momentum and excitement which sweeps the candidate off their feet. It's about a mindset which has the same laser focus as winning a big new customer order. Some call it "closing the deal". How can we harness and coordinate *all our resources* to land the win, how do we ensure we beat out the competition and make us the preferred option? Yes, we have to be in a good state revenue and profit-wide, yes, we need to show growth and career prospects, yes we need to have a clearly defined role and remit and set of responsibilities, yes, the pay and benefits needs to be competitive, but what's the key to unlock all that potential and get the best talent on-board?

What's this new *1-week paradigm*? It's about: organising so that once the key talent is identified, then line up the interviews and move to offer *within one week*. Overwhelm the candidate with interest, positivity and enthusiasm. Make the whole thing exciting. Use the one week to show "we can move fast" in this new tech-driven /digital world, we can be as smart as anyone and this demonstrates we really want you.

There's been many books written about "competitive advantage through people", showcasing case studies that demonstrate that people are the key assets of the organisation, that through people the company can win if the workforce is motivated and properly managed. Some companies will talk about being customer-centric and being customer-led. But the more savvy will talk about "power through people", they will see the virtuous circle that if their employees are motivated and excited and informed and care about what the company is doing, then that will naturally translate through to the way they connect and engage with customers and through that they will drive market success and advantage. In the UK, we've talked about LV and Nationwide as leading examples. And I still admire the model at retailer John Lewis which was so successful for many years and no reason why a strong and empathetic new management team could not recreate and reestablish that model where employees were embraced as "partners", sharing in the profits no matter what level they were at in the organisation fostering a sense of togetherness, sharing and belonging and wanting their company to succeed. Others like Next plc, Estee Lauder, Admiral Insurance, even the likes of Accenture and Deloitte all continue to score highly, despite their size and scale, as best places to work.

People are the key. Not surprising that there's an ongoing war for the best, and not surprising that GAFA companies, being born in the Tech age with an entrepreneurial mindset, have been able to adopt and embrace a best practice approach from day 1.

We all read nowadays about how companies should become more agile, how they should move from linear thinking to agile ways of working, So GAFA have embraced that ideal in their talent acquisition process. It's not any more about let's set up the first interview, see how that goes, then set up the next one, and then after that let's do another. Now instead, the process is as follows:

Day 1 Monday: meet a top talent for the first time, if like what you meet.
Day 2: Tuesday: call first thing, invite back in
Day 3: Wednesday: line up 5 interviews all on the same day
Day 4: Thursday: **make offer**, invite to come in /meet the team, send contract by email end of day
Day 5 Friday: end of day drinks with all the interviewers, **shake hands, sign.**

Day 5 is "close the deal day". What do we have to do to get this person on-board? Let's see if we can capture the week's momentum, let's keep the buzz, nothing more powerful than having this person back with us, offer letter on the table, a "signing ceremony", it doesn't have to be done shyly and privately behind closed doors, let's imagine it's like a star footballer signing their new contract in front of the world's press and photographers. We can make a show of it and in doing so show how much we want this person to join.

And yes, the offer letter can be subject to references and contain 3-month probation clauses to give the company added security and safeguard but in principle we all want to go home Friday evening with the deal closed, the job done, this brilliant new talent signed-up.

★ ★ ★

Why don't all companies operate in this way? Why do many especially large organisations take months and months to go through a process of interviews and consideration? Is it any wonder that such companies with such a process may lose out on the best?

In recent times my recruitment work has seen a step-change in the level of interest and demand for example in Data, Ai/Analytics and Insight roles. Whether as Chief Data Officer, or Director of Analytics, or Head of Ai and Data Science, companies all now can see the value that good data management can bring to underpin more effective customer engagement, revenue development and pricing decision-making.

As an example, one recent client of mine is a FTSE 100 Financial Services organisation. They created a new role which was to be their Chief Data Officer. The role was seen as important enough for the organisation that it would it report direct to the CEO and potentially could become a main Board position.

The company had talked about the need for urgency, they recognised there is a lot of demand for the best talent in this space, how it was imperative to move quickly, how this would be a high profile appointment for the company and so important to get the best.

A shortlist of candidates, identified, checked and ready to meet was completed in less than 3 weeks. However, this is what the company did next:

Week 1: meet the shortlist of candidates
Week 2: evaluate and consider and review feedback internally
Week 3: identify top 3 to move forward with
Week 4: get back with next step dates /meeting options for 2 weeks' time
Week 6: second-round interviews
Week 7: review internal feedback
Week 8: decide on top 2 to move forward with
Week 10: third-round interviews

…and so on…with final interview at the end of 3 months.

Guess what happened? The final candidate gets an offer from the client but that same week they get approached by a GAFA company.

One week later candidate has a new offer to consider, and it's exciting. "these guys moved really quickly, they really showed they wanted me, they're putting quite a lot of pressure on me to accept this week, I've been invited back in later today for a drinks /more informal meeting with the interviewers, I'll let you know how that goes…

In the end the company did get their person. But it was touch and go for a couple of weeks while the candidate was getting to know a new quick Agile and fast-moving company and comparing that with the slower more traditional pace and wondering what that said about the two companies and ways of working and potential at each.

The good news is that not only did the client company eventually win-out but they also wanted to learn and understand what is was that the GAFA company was doing and how was it able to move so quickly.

The company has now established a new "top talent" interview process". They felt that adopting the 1-week paradigm was at this stage perhaps too big a jump for them. But what about 1-month? It would not be the fastest but it would represent a step-change in their speed and agility and in doing so give the company a much better of chance of securing the top talent it wanted in the future.

To underpin that a new dashboard was established which would help the HR and Talent Acquisition teams to measure and monitor how efficiently they were able to manage the recruitment process:

Key recruitment KPI:
- *Time from brief to offer*
- *Time from first interview to offer*
- *Time from offer to close*
- *Number of interviews*
- *% of interviews on same day*
- *% offers accepted*

★ ★ ★

What can recruiters and headhunters do to facilitate this? One easy solution is to speed up their own process. It's no longer acceptable to spend 2 or 3 weeks indulging in "mapping the market" and then another 3 or 4 weeks while the recruiting firm trawls that market. That can mean 6 weeks or more from brief before the company even sees sight of an early shortlist.

This new "1-week paradigm" requires a fast approach from the off. In my recruiting work, I commit to get the shortlist within 2 to 3 weeks maximum. I don't waste time briefing junior researchers, I am able to leverage many years personal experience and networks and get straight to potential candidates on day 1 after the brief. By the end of week 1, I can already have the start of the shortlist ready to go. All that means momentum, speed and agility and the ability to get the process up and running very quickly. I'm finding that can make a significant difference as I only work on one role at a time, so all my efforts and energies are dedicated to getting to the best candidates and getting them excited and ready to interview.

★ ★ ★

In today's fast-moving world, no process can be complete and no new ways of working can guarantee success. But it's clear that to capture the best talent in the market, companies do have to learn to move more quickly, to develop that GAFA-like buzz and excitement with the candidate that ensures they are keen and ready to sign-up and join. It can come down to the simple process changes described here that any organisation can adopt and give itself the best chance of success.

Chapter 13

Using the recruitment process to benchmark candidates and resolve uncertainty

There are many studies now pointing to a shortage of Digital and Data skills, more demand than quality supply, as companies race to find and build the best talent pools and teams. With the war for talent getting ever more competitive, so companies are having to become more flexible in the way they consider recruiting and the speed that they move ahead.

A recent Gartner survey pointed out that one of the common roadblocks which gets in the way of quickly and effectively building digital and data teams is "uncertainty".

They found that execs often delay because they are unsure of what talent they need. They are not certain about the precise skills profile, job specs take a long time to finalise and there is disagreement about timing, location and reporting lines. And this "disagreement" can drag on for a long time. For example, is a User Experience expert best reporting to Marketing or to IT, should e-Commerce candidates report into Operations or Marketing, should Heads of Data report into IT or Finance or Marketing or given their importance to driving future success perhaps direct into the CEO?

All these are legitimate questions and concerns but they can take months to resolve and often end up in unsatisfactory compromise. There is however an alternative. Instead of trying to decide these issues in theory, better to identify in practice. And for a number of leading companies now like Novartis, Adobe, Aviva, Barclays, Intel and others, the answer lies in using the recruiting process *"to meet and learn"*.

This means using the process very deliberately to meet a range of prospective candidates for a specific role. Let's say it's a Head of Digital. So the company can work with a recruiter to find such candidates and deliberately choose to consider applicants from different targeted backgrounds. Some may have come up through the IT ranks, some through Marketing, some through Customer Operations and Experience. But the idea is: let's meet a sample of such candidates, let's arrange for the say 3 key internal stakeholders to meet that sample, and through that process, through meeting and interview, through questioning and getting to know different candidates, so let's use that to help us determine what the right sort of profile is and so crystalise what we do need, *and what we don't*, what is the right sort of background and profile that will work for us, our culture, our business needs and our organisation.

This recruitment process is set up with the clear recognition that it may indeed not lead to a final hire. But what it will do is provide the empirical, in-market insight and evidence and end the uncertainty and the continued internal and somewhat theoretical debate.

If it should lead to a hire then all the better. But an alternative and very satisfactory outcome can be to shortcut months of debate and uncertainty, align around the right candidate profile, clarify and confirm the focus and goals of the job spec and be able then to quickly go back to the market with a clear brief and clear knowledge of exactly what looking for. And that can lead to a quick and very rewarding hiring process for all.

This sort of recruitment process, to learn about the candidate market, and to resolve internal uncertainties, has been pioneered by those GAFA companies (Google, Amazon, Facebook and Apple) that we reviewed in the last chapter. They will often use this approach and method as their Stage 1 recruiting process. They are very clear with the candidates from the outset as to what they are looking to achieve. And for candidates it can also be an attractive way to get to know an organisation, establish contact, get a foot in the door and if not this role, then be on the radar screen at the company in case something more suitable and relevant comes up in the future.

So it can be win:win and why not. With the talent war set to become even more intense then companies must use every opportunity to move ahead, cut out the delaying factors and be able to find and capture key talent at speed.

Chapter 14

Spotify – case study

Spotify was set up in 2006, a leading Swedish company, rapidly achieving global reach and market leadership, it has been widely viewed as an organisation model that can work well for companies grappling with the need for ongoing change and transformation. It has its advocates and also its detractors but it's worth re-considering as companies look to adapt to an age which is increasingly all about Technology.

Recent times has also seen some challenges at Spotify itself, so no matter how well it has organised it's not immune from macro-economic market conditions and levels of competition in its market place. Founder/CEO Daniel Ek consistently takes a positive outlook on the company's prospects and has recently updated the markets on their next 3-5 year strategy and plan to be fit for their next wave of growth:

In Spotify's early days, our success was hard won. We had limited resources and had to make the most of every asset. Our ingenuity and creativity and the way we organised ourselves were what set us apart.

The Spotify of tomorrow must be defined by being relentlessly resourceful in the ways we operate, innovate, and tackle problems. This kind of resourcefulness transcends the basic definition – it's about preparing for our next phase, where being lean and efficient puts us in the best position.

This will be the next stage in our organisation evolution and will also allow us to invest our profits more strategically back into the business. With a more targeted approach, every investment and initiative becomes more impactful, offering greater opportunities for success. We're still committed to investing and making bold bets, but now, with a more focused approach, ensuring Spotify's continued profitability and ability to innovate. This means smarter, more impactful paths to achieve our ambitions.

A true evolution in how we operate our company, a year where we started to prove that we're not just a company that has an amazing product, but one that also continuing to build a great business.

How does Spotify organise itself to exploit its market opportunities and build its business?

Its more than 9,000 employees are organized into agile teams, called squads, which are self-organizing, cross-functional, and co-located. Spotify has largely succeeded in maintaining an agile mindset and principles without sacrificing accountability. It enables innovation while keeping the benefits of repeatability, and it creates alignment without excessive control. Some of its lessons can potentially apply to many companies, not just digitally enabled service providers.

Spotify's core organizational unit is an autonomous squad of no more than ten people. Each squad is accountable for a discrete aspect of the product, which it owns cradle to grave. Squads have the authority to decide what to build, how to build it, and with whom to work to make the product interoperable. They are organised into a light matrix called a tribe. Tribes comprise several squads linked together through a chapter, which is a horizontal grouping that helps to support specific competencies such as quality assistance, agile coaching, and web development. The chapter's primary role is to facilitate learning and competency development throughout the squads.

Leadership within the squad is self-determined, while the chapter leader is a formal manager who focuses on coaching and mentoring. Spotify believes in the player-coach model: Chapter leaders are also squad members. Squad members can switch squads and retain the same formal leader within their chapter. Spotify introduced a third organisational element, known as a guild. Guilds are lightweight communities of interest whose primary purpose is to share knowledge in areas that cut across chapters and squads, such as leadership, continuous development, and web delivery.

This unusual combination of squads, tribes, chapters, and guilds is the organisational infrastructure that underlies Spotify's operating model. At first reading, it might sound like just another way to define a conventional organisational matrix in digital/tech friendly terms. But a closer examination reveals just how different the model really is and why it seems to work so well.

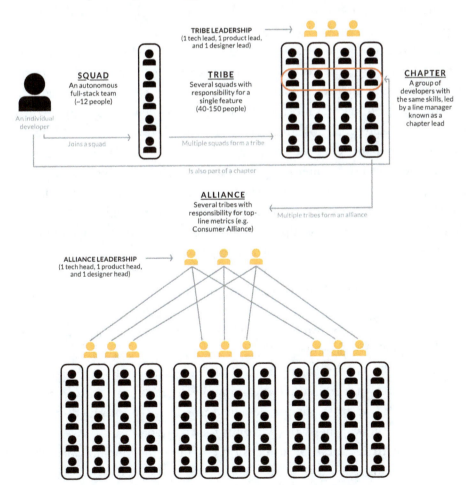

The squad structure works in teams no bigger than 10 and even as Spotify has grown it helps the company still feel small and manageable. The squads are fully autonomous and 100% responsible for a single feature. In a way it's seen as having lots of small start-ups (squads) that harness the power of the bigger company by combining expertise (guilds and chapters) while creating alignment through tribes and alliances.

The squad structure achieves autonomy without sacrificing accountability. Every squad owns its features throughout the product's life cycle, and the squads have full visibility into their features' successes and failures. There is no single appointed leader of a squad; any such leadership role is emergent and informal. Results are visible both through internal reviews and through customer feedback, and squads are expected to fully understand successes and failures. Squads go through end of term analyses of failures to ensure learning, and some squad rooms have "fail walls." Every few weeks, squads conduct retrospectives to evaluate what is going well and what needs to improve.

To ensure that the feedback process is effective for individuals as well as for the squads, Spotify redesigned its performance management system to separate salary discussion and performance evaluations from coaching and feedback. Before, peer feedback was incorporated into salary reviews; in Spotify's words, that "incentivised people to gather as many favourable reviews as possible rather than getting feedback around their biggest areas of potential improvement." Now, colleagues use an internal tool to invite anyone — including managers, peers, and direct reports — to provide feedback on results and on what an individual can do to improve. Employees may solicit feedback as often as they choose..."the result is a process that everyone needs to own and drive themselves — it is about development and personal growth."

- **Continuous improvement:** both personally, and in the wider organisation.
- **Iterative development:** short learning cycles to validate assumptions as quickly as possible.
- **Simplicity:** Simplicity is the mantra guidance during scaling for methods of working and organising the organisation.
- **Trust:** "we trust our people and teams to make informed decisions about the way they work and what they work on."
- **Servant leadership:** a focus on coaching, mentorship, and solving problems rather than telling people what to do.

Culture plays a big role in keeping the innovation engine firing on all cylinders. Spotify has an experiment-friendly culture with an emphasis on test-and-learn approaches and contained experiments. If people don't know the best way to do something, they are likely to try alternative approaches and run several A/B tests to determine which is preferable. In place of opinion, ego, and authority, Spotify say they work hard to substitute data, experimentation, and open dialogue about root causes.

Spotify fosters alignment. The central organisational feature that shapes Spotify's model is the concept of "loosely coupled, tightly aligned squads." The key belief here is that "alignment enables autonomy — the greater the alignment, the more autonomy you can grant." That's why the company spends so much time aligning on objectives and goals before launching into work. The leadership model at Spotify reinforces this alignment. A leader's job is to figure out the right problem and communicate it, so that squads can collaborate to find the best solution. Coordination comes through context and through a deep understanding of the company's priorities, product strategies, and overall mission. The ability to release features and then flex them enables full releases even before all features are fully operational. Here, too, the culture acts as a support. The watchword at Spotify is "be autonomous, but don't suboptimise — be a good citizen in the Spotify ecosystem." A common analogy at the company is a jazz band: Each squad plays its instrument, but each also listens to the others and focuses on the overall piece to make great music.

Clearly, not all of Spotify's choices will be appropriate for every company. But the Spotify approach is a benchmark which seems to work well for them and an example as to how companies can change the way they organise to be able to move at pace and impact in this digital world. Companies need to make explicit choices in their operating model, ways of working, and culture that can address core tensions between individual autonomy and organisational goals. The goal is to get alignment without excessive control and at heart build an engaging and inspiring working environment.

A number of companies are now actively looking at this Spotify organisation model and wondering if this might be the next stage of their own evolution. Companies like Vodafone, Zoopla, Skyscanner and others. They admire the Spotify culture of innovation and fast pace market development, they can see how that has helped the company grow fast and drive to a global market leadership, they see that people in the company appear genuinely committed to it and to its future success. They care. So companies wonder, can we implement the same sort of model?

But when companies do copy the 'Spotify model', it can sometimes happen through a top-down directive, without perhaps taking a close enough look at what kind of culture and leadership is needed to make it work.

Often the existing structure is simply changed, overnight, into a new matrix blueprint, an organisation model that is suddenly labelled with Squads, Chapters, and Tribes and with some expectation and notion that this will transform the company into a fast-paced high-growth innovative and dynamic organisation which will barnstorm to market leadership. Instead of, perhaps, looking at culture and ways of working and growing an evolutionary structure that's right for a particular organisation and is able to take-on a change agenda.

Implementing a Spotify solution, as some large established corporations seem to be doing, can work but there have been examples for example at Vodafone where it has created confusion and complexity. It might be right for a 50-person start-up, or for a highly entrepreneurial organisation born in the Technology age, but for a large legacy multi-national corporation with multiple systems and processes, it could be a high cost and high risk move.

Just as startups like Spotify found the right organisation culture and model *for them,* so every organisation needs to find its own "organisation-fit". That might involve adopting some elements of this Spotify solution, or even all of it, but only after careful check and examination.

"Stop trying to borrow wisdom and think for yourself. Face your difficulties and think and think and think and solve your problems yourself. Suffering and difficulties provide opportunities to become better. Success is never giving up."

-from Taiichi Ohno, a leading Japanese organisation /operations engineer, the "father" of Lean Manufacturing

Chapter 15

Building the digital team

Why are some companies being especially successful in this digital tech world?

What about Shein.com for example. It effectively started in China in 2010 and has become by some measures, the largest global online only fashion company.

It is now the leader of a new generation of fast fashion that is out-manoeuvring and outpacing longer established rivals like Zara and H&M, producing thousands of new items to match the current trends every week. On an average day, Shein adds 2,000 new items to its store.

At the time of writing, Shein generated $22.7 billion in revenues, a 44% increase on the year before. It has an estimated 88.8 million active shoppers, 17.3 million are based in the US

Shein is downloaded 200 million times in a year, making it most downloaded shopping app. It was recently valued at $68 billion.

Take some other examples: Kraft Foods launched a new product line "tapping into online social media and influencers", *South Beach*, which achieved $100m of sales in 1 year, RELX Group plc migrated from being a print publisher to a highly regarded digital information software business doubling market cap in 5 years, Monzo Bank founded in 2015 is rated as the leading UK online/ digital bank with revenues of c. £350m and more than 7 million customers, voted Best Banking App and Best for Service & Quality, how is that Amazon also built up so quickly and still today continues to increase its extraordinary market sector penetration and customer engagement? What are these types of companies doing to exploit the new, still fast-changing digital landscape and achieve that winning market position?

The answer lies in how they organise for digital tech, how they build their teams and their skills sets, how they develop a culture inside that is supportive and encouraging of digital technology innovation and development, how they share and learn, how they attract and retain key talent who can make the difference. They've got Digital Tech into their mainstream, into their DNA, they realise its importance but most critically they act and behave and implement and deliver and reward for digital initiative and success.

There are 6 key decisions that need to get made if a company is to join these digital tech winners. These are around:

1. *Structure and Organisation*
2. *Leadership and Engine room*
3. *Skills and Scale*
4. *Culture and Style*
5. *Learning and Sharing*
6. *Talent Finding and Retaining*

Let's look at each in turn. Before we do it's worth reminding of the Facebook/Meta mantra that is written large on the walls of their office: "The journey is *just 1% finished*".

The Facebook/Meta leadership recognise and appreciate that "we've only just begun in our ambitions and what can be achieved". And it is a journey, not just for Facebook, but for all companies. The technology landscape continues to change at breath-taking speed, it's hard for any individual or company to keep up, the boundaries of what's possible and what is not keep changing, the potential for disruption in the market is never-ending, new possibilities and potential in existing and in new markets are surfacing all the time. This "technology revolution" that we are living through is still in its early stages. And just as the market place keeps evolving, so the journey for companies stretches out into time as an organisation tries to assimilate and absorb and process what all these changes may mean for its future, for what to invest in, what to prioritise, what skills and organisation shape and what technology changes required to capture these market opportunities and deliver continued shareholder value.

Many companies struggle with all the change opportunities, want to leapfrog and jump to some higher technical plane, but while that ambition may be laudable, it needs to come with the recognition that it does all take time. Leapfrogging for an established corporation is hard to do, in fact it's difficult for any company to make successful changes and even step-changes in the way it operates. So what's critical is, yes have the ambition for sure, have the clear goals and sense of mission and purpose. But put that into the context of what can the organisation cope with, how ready is it for change, what external catalysts and support and hiring is required to enable and facilitates these changes, what's the right timeframe and timetable that allows for the current business operations to keep going and developing even while new ways of working and new levels of customer engagement take shape and can begin to make their impact.

1. Structure and organisation

A common question is: should we keep Digital as a separate stand-alone team and group or should we simply have it all somehow integrated into the core of the company?

Digital started off in every organisation as a separate group and team. There were these specialist skills such as Search engine optimisation, SEO and SEM, and such people were often pioneers, evangelists, sometimes technical geeks who did things and seemed to know things that others in the company barely understood but had been convinced were nevertheless somehow important for their customers. And of course, that "specialist" digital unit started to grow adding other skills such as "front end web developers", content writers, web designers, email marketers, web analysts... Over a short space of time a few specialists, at least in the larger organisations became a large team. And what's more, instead of just managing a bit of online brochureware, they were starting to drive ever larger chunks of revenue. Suddenly this team became the growth engine of the company.

At retailer John Lewis for example, so specialist and important did this team become, that they had their own offices in a separate building with its own team managers, culture, ways of working and doing its own thing, a mystery and black box to the rest of the organisation, more than 150 people, somehow though justifying themselves as they drew more and more plaudits from commentators and customers and became responsible for a sizeable percentage of the JL business.

For JL, there came a point where this mystery had gone on too long. There was a felt need to learn, to absorb, to transfer this customer and market know-how and get the whole organisation on-board with this way of thinking and engaging with customers. So the separate office was shut, the digital team was brought back into the head office, front end developers were reconnected with the IT team, online marketers were made a part of the wider company Marketing team, people were integrated. But still not completely. There is still a Head of Online and Digital who manages eg the specialist online marketers. That Head of Online may report to the equivalent of the CMO, but the digital team have still kept their distinctiveness and the organisation is forced to acknowledge that however much it may desire complete integration, that that goal today is just not possible, that there is need for specialists with particular skills and expertise. Yes make sure what they do is part of the overall long term customer vision and plan, but accept too that they need to move and innovate and operate often in a distinctive style and way and need to be given the scope to test and trial new market place ideas all the time.

This John Lewis vignette is mirrored in many other companies today. Should we leave the specialists to get on with it, or, if we "bring them back in", then will we lose that expertise and dilute the market potential? On the other hand, doesn't the whole organisation need to be working to an integrated multi-channel agenda? Shouldn't everyone be somehow involved now in this tech-led world?

To answer this question, it's critical to acknowledge and respect that each and every organisation is different. Every company is at different stages of its digital journey. If Facebook feel they are only at 1% then where are the long established corporations? Are the likes of eg Shell or Philips or Procter & Gamble still only at the starting gate? Or has each in its own way in fact been effectively laying the foundations and building the capabilities that will enable it to succeed in a digital world? Each company has different culture, style and ways of thinking, each is at its own state of digital maturity and readiness and that as much as anything will determine and define how it organises and how it evolves, what it keeps specialist and what it integrates. But for most every company, the vision of a fully integrated, "we are all now digital" environment and organisation structure is still a long way off.

To help understand how any one particular organisation should structure its digital teams, the following sections can add further perspective on how others are doing it and what needs to be considered in making the decision.

2. Leadership and engine room

Who should lead the Digital Tech charge? It's now become so critical to so many companies' futures, that it has become a c-suite role. We now see an ever-growing number of "Chief Digital Officers" being appointed. This can reflect the growing recognition of just how much of the company's business is now dependent on being successful in this space.

This "elevation" of digital to the senior ranks has at the same time brought a number of tensions, especially in the relationship of the CDO with the CMO and CIO (too many "c's"?).

For example, who is responsible for the customer? Historically that responsibility would naturally have been the remit of the CMO. But if there is a CDO and eg half the revenues are online, then shouldn't perhaps the CDO have equal responsibility? And if so how does that "responsibility" get shared, who makes the final call?

This can get even more complicated where online becomes the majority of the business. If the CDO has P&L responsibility and is acknowledged as being the leader of that, then why is there a need for a separate group CEO, shouldn't the CDO in effect become the CEO?

All this is just a further illustration of the still relative immaturity of digital, or put another way, it's an example of where most companies are on their journey that this sort of issue is only just beginning to surface and has not yet been answered or addressed.

While this leadership battle rages away, there is also a next level challenge in the engine room. That is how best to organise and structure the digital teams, the key junior execs and mid-level managers who are building and driving and nurturing the business day by day. Part of this question is also where best to locate them. Is it a John Lewis type solution, should they remain separate, should they be integrated and if integrated then just how much!

One way of resolving this is to look at 3 companies by way of example, who have each adopted a similar structure. The 3 are Amazon.com, Costa Coffee and Next, the clothing retail group.

Each of these vanguard companies has realised how important it is to get its web sites and online presence optimised. They have realised that this is not a once-a-year review, but needs to be something continuous and ongoing, ideally 24/7 and if possible in real time.

Each has responded to this challenge by restructuring and reorganising 3 specific teams. That is (i) the front end web developers, (ii) the web analytics and insight group and (iii) the online marketing team. The decision was made that these 3 groups be brought together, be co-located and sat next to each other and also report into the same person. Usually that's the Marketing Director or could be the Head of Site Optimisation or in other companies even the Chief Customer Officer.

The web analytics team are constantly monitoring user journeys, fall out rates, which promotional offers are working and which are not, should a promotion be ended now, should the price be reduced or raised, should a call to action be made more prominent, put in a different colour, put in a different place on the web site, what's being said about the company, the products on social media, is any response needed, what else is happening externally with the weather, politics, sport, internationally that might influence or change what might work today, this hour, this minute online that could optimise the customer experience and maximise sales.

The web analytics team are identifying these change opportunities in real time, they share that with the Marketing /Commercial team who are charged with making immediate decisions on what to change if anything in response to the observed insights.

The front end web dev team then take over and make the changes, fast.

All this delivers a highly responsive, targeted, customised, digital operations environment that is looking at all that's going on, on desktop and mobile, and fine-tuning with agility and speed.

It is that type of "engine room" management and structuring that can make a tremendous difference to a company's success.

3. Skills and scale

A significant challenge is how to afford the wide variety of specialists required to deliver the Digital potential. There seem to be any number of very distinct skill sets ranging through the value chain from Customer Awareness development through Customer Engagement and Conversion and then keeping them coming back!

The skills need necessarily to include some or all of SEO, SEM, online media display, affiliates, content, social media, creative design, conversion, analytics, e-commerce /transaction management, CRM, fulfilment, returns, technical web development, project management, mobile, partnerships and intermediaries, product /service strategy, roadmap and innovation…

Some companies just don't have the size and scale of budgets to afford to bring in specialists for each one of these areas. Many other companies do have the scale and budget potential but have other priorities or just don't appreciate and realise the need and value potential or have other pressures on costs and people.

The typical compromise is to bring in a few and ask them to multi-task, to work across the whole digital value chain and do their best to optimise where possible. Such an approach may be a fiscal necessity but it's important that an organisation does appreciate what skills it does *not* have and so adjusts its targets and expectations accordingly.

For some others, the solution involves bringing in contractors and freelancers for a particular project only and justifying that resource on the back of a specific project RoI. That can work well though clearly individuals hired on that temporary basis will sometimes lack the emotional engagement with the product and brand and the genuine desire and passion to go the extra mile to make this succeed.

An alternative solution is to set up a network of support agencies and consultancies who can advise and take on specific projects eg rebuild the web site.

Whatever the solution path that is chosen, it should be part of a long term strategy that looks at the role digital can play in an organisation and looks at a gradual build up in budgets and people and capabilities. Taking a purely year by year approach that is at best incremental and perhaps squeezes a 5% increase in spend and activity is unlikely to match the pace of change in the company's market place and the readiness of customers to embrace any digital initiatives the company does make.

B2B companies have been especially "guilty" of this slow incremental approach, looking at the slow pace of their competitors and using that to justify their own inactivity. But many such organisations have found that if they do invest and create an effective digital marketplace for their customers then it can have a significant impact and gets a surprisingly quick and positive customer response. Companies like Cisco, Intel, BP, Coats plc, BT, Pitney Bowes have all discovered that if they do divert resources and spend to Digital then *it does pay back.*

4. Culture and style

Successful digital-led companies have developed 3 core elements to their culture:

- fostering an entrepreneurial spirit
- creating an agile environment of "test, trial and learn"
- recognising that we are going through an era of fast change and that there will be ambiguity and uncertainty and that that is ok!

The best digital people are often pioneers, they thrive on change, they look for adventure and the chance to explore possibilities, they aren't comfortable working in an environment where everything is set, where there's little room for manoeuver, they want to work fast and get things done, and not wait 6 months for IT to change some copy on the web site. They are more instinctively entrepreneurs, they thrive where that spirit is fostered and supported, they are comfortable with change and actually are prepared to push for that, ambiguity does not unsettle or discomfort them, on the contrary that is what they expect and what enables them to think and act and come up with disruptive solutions that can be game-changers.

In today's world, a winning business needs these sort of people in its midst. Such individuals can also help shift the whole corporate culture to a more focussed 21st century business model.

5. Learning and sharing

Hyper Island is one of the world's leading learning and training centres for Digital. Its 3 day "Digital Masterclass" is almost legendary in its ability to convert doubting or uncertain execs into overnight digital evangelists. It's set up for groups of senior execs but can also be used at all levels across the company. There are usually around 30 in the class group and it's a full 3 day immersion, staying overnight, working hard in both lectures and workshops and presentations that share what others are achieving and driving out what could be possible.

Less a "class" than an introduction to a new way of thinking, it's intended as an intensive immersion and learning and there are other groups that do this as well including the major business schools like MIT, Columbia and INSEAD but the Hyper Island can appeal as it's more "short sharp e-shock".

There are also any number of seminars and conferences that seek to train and share best practices and latest ideas eg at the IDM (Institute of Direct Marketing) and at CIM (Chartered Institute of Marketing). For those who want to dig deeper there are longer training programmes such as the MSc (a part time /evenings /remote learning programme) in Internet Retailing at Manchester Metropolitan University and coordinated by e-Consultancy.

These courses do not just appeal to those who wish to learn. They also have a pivotal role where a group of execs in a company are trying to drive through digital change and technology innovation and encountering resistance and hesitation from colleagues whose support they need. If such colleagues can be persuaded to participate in some external education and enlightenment, then it can of course change the pace and direction of the company's development and investment.

This need for immersion, learning and training, for sharing ideas and expertise is all the more critical in the digital world. Things are moving fast, they are changing, new more agile start-up ventures are springing up out of nowhere challenging incumbents and disrupting decades long and traditional ways of thinking and operating. Innovations may be customer-facing but they can also be internal process-driven enabling eg lower costs of production or automating processes which can speed up time to market. It's near impossible to do the day job and stay up-to-date on all the potential disruptive forces at work, so sharing, training, listening to experts, finding, somehow, that occasional time to listen and learn, creating the environment at work which both encourages and enables that, that can all lay the foundations for a successful future.

6. Talent finding and retaining

Many say that they find it very difficult to attract key digital talent. They may find it takes months, perhaps even 6 to 9 months to find someone. In some cases, companies give up on that targeted hire altogether. They either make do, or have to reach out to some agency or consultancy to provide the resource and support.

Yet some companies have it seems no problem at all in quickly attracting the right sort of candidate profile. Whether it's a new venture like Shein.com, a complex audit /advisory group like Deloitte, a B2B publisher like Incisive, manufacturer distributors like Coats plc, Smith & Nephew or the likes of Tesco and Next.

How do companies develop that talent attraction? The 7 simple keys are:

(i)   A good quality online presence so that when the candidate looks up the company for the first time they get a good impression,

(ii)   A good "digital tech story", a good explanation available as to where the company is on its digital journey, a recognition that there is a long way still to go, a sense of that adventure and what the goals are,

(iii)   A commitment to digital technology and transformation from the CEO and through-out the corporation,

(iv)   A readiness to invest, even modestly, in new ideas

(v)   A fast-paced interview process that takes weeks not months

(vi)   A reasonable amount of flexibility around the job spec so as not to exclude good, bright, fast-learning people who may not be able to tick all the boxes yet on the spec.

(vii)   Flexibility, within reason, on pay and benefits.

Sometimes it may just eg need a small sign-on to compensate an exec for loss of bonus accrued at previous employ or need to buy a season ticket for the longer commute.

It just requires a readiness and desire to move quickly, be flexible and make it easy for the right candidates to say yes!

Another way of thinking about this is to reflect on the prospective employee "user journey". There's lots of talk and effort going into to the optimisation of the customer journey to maximise conversion. Much less attention has been paid to the *employee* experience and how that can be optimised to streamline hiring and make acceptance easy.

From the first contact to the last and then through to the on-boarding process, who in the company is responsible? HR initiate and coordinate but they require the hiring managers to do their bit and make time available, not cancel interviews at the last minute, give immediate feedback, be prepared properly for the interviews, recognise that for the candidate this can be a life-changing moment and so treat that moment with the respect it deserves.

Too often, even for relatively junior roles, there can be 6 to 12 interviews (in one case I know of 24!). It is of course almost impossible that a candidate will be liked by everyone they see. Does one "no" outweigh 9 "yes's"? That can often be the case. And as each interview is set up, so the timetable is drawn out, the weeks turn into months and meantime a faster-moving company comes in and snaps up the prospective hire.

Getting this right helps get the right candidate on board. But then they also need to be retained. Good digital people are on every recruiter's radar screen. They may just have moved jobs but they're still getting calls about new opportunities. So if the new job does not live up to expectations they can be seduced and intrigued by something elsewhere, "the grass is greener?"

★ ★ ★

By way of a summary, we can review the following Barclays case study, looking at how the Bank has become more "digital first".

From pioneering CEO Ashok Vaswani came a stream of communications about digital. His mantra: "Digitization is redefining and transforming our business".

This has included a wide number of initiatives. The target has been to educate the workforce and turn each and every employee into a digital evangelist. And through that galvanise and engage customers in a more digital-designed way. Vaswani's goal was for employees to become more digitally literate, to bring about new ways to connect with customers, to identify new business and revenue streams and to take advantage of new technologies.

Internally, people were encouraged to dress more comfortably, the work space was changed to include pods and chill-out areas, football tables appeared!, ties disappeared, seminars were held with the idea of teaching everyone about why digital is important and what that would mean.

Employees were encouraged to become "digital natives" and to participate in various training programmes inside the bank and externally too. "Reverse mentors" were set up, throughout the bank, so that senior execs were deliberately exposed to latest digital ideas and diplomatically encouraged to change ways of operating. The Bank launched its high profile Digital Eagles consumer publicity campaign ensuring that each and every branch had its own digital champion who could encourage consumers to use the newly installed self-serve machines rather than stand in line and wait for counter service. 12000 Digital Eagles have so far been trained to evangelise at branch level. Alongside this, is the Barclays Digital Code Playground, a widely-advertised initiative to encourage people to come to "learn to code" training sessions run for free in the Bank's local branches.

What does all this mean? It starts to change a whole culture across a huge and sprawling organisation. The employees feel the need to be a part of this as it starts to become an accelerated route for promotion and higher bonus levels.

It showcases the Bank in a different light to a perhaps cynical or sceptical public who begin to change their perception of what Barclays can do for them.

Banks are unlikely to ever have a warm cuddly brand image, they're not going to be like a Marks and Spencer, but they can move with the times, they can change what they stand for, they can use digital to streamline how they organise and operate, they can look for new ways of working that will make it easy for customers to use their services online and by mobile, they can create an environment where employees feel there is opportunity and adventure and that things are moving forward, they can help make themselves seen as the leading employer for digital services in the financial services sector, they can look to be a future winner and leave other rivals behind.

Chapter 16

How to structure and organise the digital team

Digital Value Chain

Recent research from McKinsey shows a key agenda item is all around: *how should companies best organise to capture the increasingly critical digital tech opportunity?*

Some 63% in a recent survey said that they were unsure how to structure and fit digital tech skills into their existing teams. 31% felt that it was now requiring a totally new look at skills, teams, reporting lines and ways of working. 27% also commented that "integrating new digital talent" was proving "surprisingly difficult!"

So what's causing this challenge and uncertainty? No-one doubts the importance of digital. Most every company, whether B2C or B2B, has seen how customers are demanding an increasingly online, automated, self-serve environment, how the customer expectation has rapidly developed for a seamless, integrated multi-channel experience, how getting that customer experience right can genuinely add incremental revenue and growth. So the need for people with digital tech skills and talent to drive this is clear.

The challenge seems to lie in the sheer size and range of new skills that a company must now embrace. Should we hire in all these different skills or can we focus on just a few, how can we budget for all this, can we see a way to get a return on this investment, how add these skills to the organisation while not upsetting the existing and still successful traditional routes to market and the people, experience and capabilities that go with that?

All the current advice on this seems to stay at the macro 30,000 feet level. It tries to answer questions like should there be a Chief Digital Officer, should digital report to the CMO or the CTO, should digital stand alone as a separate function or should it be integrated into one total group? But there's little or no advice below those big questions. They are still important but once they've been decided then how organise the next level down? How structure the junior and mid-level managers and their teams? Where do they fit in?

This chapter sets out a possible solution for this. It looks below the Director level, below the CMO or the CTO or the CDO! It takes a view as to how to organise the key skills at the coalface, the experts who are doing the detailed digital and multi-channel campaign, customer and business development.

To help with this we can identify a series of key principles and guiding criteria:

(i)   *Set up the structure with no more than 6 direct reports to the c-Level exec in charge.*

(ii)   *Keep it simple and manageable*

(iii)   *Make it measurable!*

(iv)   *Set things up in a multi-channel way so that that digital is integrated and not separated.*

(v)   *Establish the team so that together they can take one holistic and seamless view of their customer.*

(vi)   *Identify the key metrics and targets that can drive|to a clear RoI on the persons or teams hired*

(vii)   *Keep it flexible: digital is evolving fast and areas like content, social media, mobile and self-serve are becoming increasingly key drivers of success. They may at some point deserve and require more prominence in the team structure.*

Recent studies from WPP's Kantar Group and also my own D-360 on-the-ground experience show that this desired digital and multi-channel skills set can best be categorised or structured into 6 key skill areas. We can describe those categories as forming the *"multi-channel value chain"*.

The 6 key areas are:

- **Strategy** (that includes Brand and Product strategy and road-mapping)
- **Brand Awareness**
- **Consideration** (eg the content, social media, collateral that the prospective purchaser considers)
- **Lead Generation** (getting people onto the web site or eg into the call centre)
- **Conversion** (getting the sale)
- **Retention** (getting the customer to come back /make the next purchase, the "customer lifetime value").

We can map this out in this way.

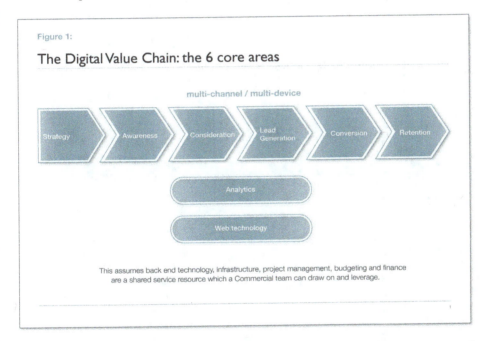

Figure 1:

The Digital Value Chain: the 6 core areas

multi-channel / multi-device

Strategy → Awareness → Consideration → Lead Generation → Conversion → Retention

Analytics

Web technology

This assumes back end technology, infrastructure, project management, budgeting and finance are a shared service resource which a Commercial team can draw on and leverage.

What we are looking at here is in effect the 6 key "Heads of Department" who would report into the c-Level Exec. They may each be directors in their own right. Or they may be "heads of" depending on size and type of company, resources and budgets and ultimately the level of ambition that the total company has. It's all about getting digital /multi-channel working at its most powerful and deliver its greatest potential.

So what's in each of these 6 departments or teams and why distinguish these 6 particular categories and stages in the value chain?

We can list out (Figure.2) the key areas of skill, remit, task and responsibility that each of these team heads can be expected to cover. The chart /table here is not intended to be exhaustive and it's certainly not a job profile. But it is a high level view of what can be expected and what's involved.

And this listing helps reinforce why these 6 distinct team areas have been defined and identified. It is because each area is specialist in its own right. Each does require particular and specific skills and expertise. Someone for example who is expert on UX may not also be expert at Product Strategy development. Equally, someone who is engaged in social media and content development will not necessarily be the best skilled person to eg drive database insight and CRM programmes. The skills are different. And to get the best from the team then the most efficient way to organise is to recognise that difference and structure accordingly.

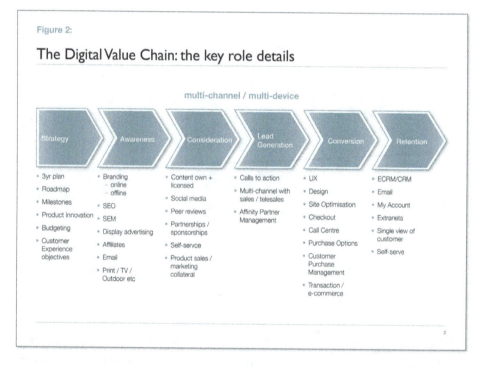

Figure 2:

The Digital Value Chain: the key role details

In early digital /multi-channel times, there was not the insight, the budgets, the returns available to start building out big teams with this sort of definition and distinction. Companies hired eg a "digital manager" and asked them to kind of oversee, well everything. Do the Search, the emails, the online advertising, the customer development, the e-commerce, the mobile app development etc. It is only in very recent times, that the scale and size of the multi-channel opportunity has grown such that this level and size of team does become possible and the RoI can be seen and quantified.

There is no question that it is a virtuous circle. Set up the team correctly, make that commitment and investment, set key goals and measures of success, target a clear RoI and drive toward that.

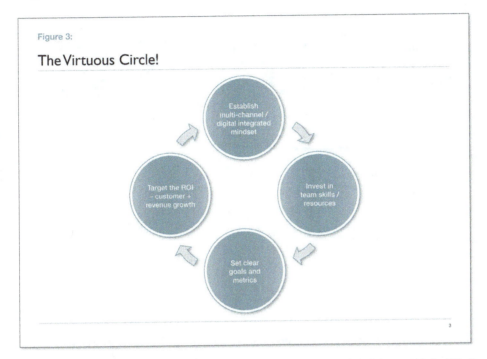

Figure 3:

The Virtuous Circle!

Establish multi-channel / digital integrated mindset

Invest in team skills / resources

Set clear goals and metrics

Target the ROI – customer + revenue growth

Figure. 4 below now shows the metrics of success, the drivers of that RoI and customer /revenue growth. It immediately shows again how very different each role is. It demonstrates clearly that a company needs its team defined and set up carefully so that there are expert people, with the right skills, able and empowered to focus on a specific set of goals.

Setting things up along these lines makes the job of the c-Level exec in charge of all this all the more manageable and achievable. That person now has 6 key reports. Each is responsible for a core and specific part of the customer multi-channel value chain. Each is tasked with a clear set of deliverables and metrics. A KPI dashboard can be set up incorporating the key metrics from each team at each stage of the chain. Success is all about getting all 6 teams to report continuing growth in their key metrics and ratios. Each is both a cost centre as well as a profit centre. If they are contributing in the right way, then their team is delivering. They can put forward investment proposals in their area and identify their potential RoI. That might be more resource or more funds or a new product /feature/service launch. But each step is therefore measurable and all the more manageable for it.

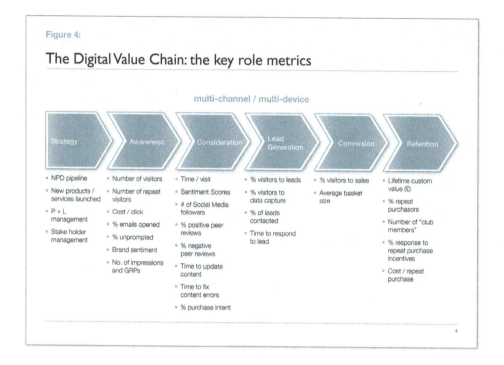

Figure 4:

The Digital Value Chain: the key role metrics

★ ★ ★

Any organisation research will always make the same observation: what is right for one company may not be right for another. Effective organisation structure depends as much as anything on the company culture, where it puts its priorities, its readiness to invest, its status on the digital /multi-channel journey, the impact that digital is having on its customer behaviour and preferences and the size of the digital prize.

In addition, investment in this area will also be driven by the c-Level team. Some teams are inherently conservative and cost conscious, they take an incremental budget /costing /next 12 months approach and will always be reluctant to add to head count unless absolutely essential. Other teams may have more flexibility because their core business is doing well or because they intuitively see the bigger 3 to 5 year picture and recognise that if they don't invest in this area now then shareholder value may start to erode significantly as they potentially struggle to compete in a digital future.

Whatever the right solution for an organisation, then it's also important to stay flexible. Digital is moving and changing as we know fast and unpredictably. No-one was able to forecast the impact of the iPhone or iPad, few today yet understand the impact of Ai on the whole Tech, Ops, Sales and Marketing processes, or the impact of digital 3D printing, or how social media is increasingly replacing paid traditional advertising, or how mobile on-the-go connectivity is replacing the desktop and laptop. It's a changing world of course and as companies organise their teams in this area it's important to constantly review the right skills and resources are in the right places!

Chapter 17

Digital evolution of marketing / marketing department organisation structures

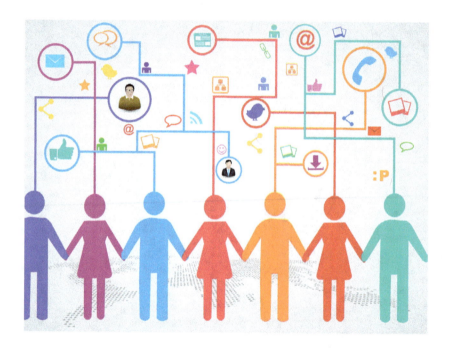

1. Background

In the good old days! Marketing was relatively straightforward to organise. Back in the 1970's when the marketing function really began to gain widespread recognition and adoption, there were typically just a few key levers that the department was responsible for. And these were mostly around building brand awareness among the target customer /consumer group.

Today's world however has become infinitely more challenging and complex. The role and responsibility of Marketing has grown significantly.

Companies today now almost universally look to their marketing team as their engine of growth. Market sectors are more competitive, they are usually global, they have become multi-channel, technology is proving disruptive while at the same time being attractive, expertise eg in digital, mobile, social, SEO is becoming more specialist and harder to obtain…getting any increase in market share and gains in revenue is just more challenging.

The progressive Marketing function however is now looking to tackle these challenges head-on. They are taking responsibility for developing the company's strategy and plans that can navigate through this market maze and develop winning solutions. The need for an integrated, multi-channel, technically literate, innovative and ever more entrepreneurial team is now becoming paramount.

This chapter looks at the evolution of the Marketing organisation. It starts with "the good old days" and looks at where things now are. There is no "right/proven" structure and model. Every company of course is different. There are differences in B2B and B2C (principally B2B have historically had less "digitally" sophisticated and developed customers, though that is also now rapidly changing!) and companies are very influenced by number of products /number of Brands, number of countries sold to, size of revenue streams, readiness of the senior directors /officers of the company to invest, how responsive the business is to new channels of communication like web, mobile, social, and just how ambitious the marketing team wants to be!

2. The good old days

There were principally two key levers: Promotions and Advertising.

The Proms team developed the annual plan and set out the promotions cycle. They would agree plans with Sales dept. about what sort of incentives required at different stage of the sales cycle. Activity would be driven mostly by the Sales team and the needs of key Trading customers. So there would be something planned for each quarter. The range of options was fairly basic, choose from direct mail, sampling, discounts and if possible eg "on-pack" competitions.

Alongside this and in support would be the *Product /Brand advertising*. This would depend on budgets and would be all about building awareness and recognition. It might be on TV or in Print or on the Radio. (Media buying and planning would invariably be outsourced to the Ad agency)

3. The 1990s

Still before the real commercial advent of the internet, yet Marketing even at this point in time was becoming significantly more sophisticated. The catalyst here was the availability of data and more and more computer processing power available on the desktop. Suddenly a marketing team could recruit in a data /insight /research team who could analyse customer behaviour, spot trends, engage in richer and deeper segmentation and identify much more tailored and refined and sophisticated marketing campaigns and activities.

So marketing teams might typically have a Head of Insight (in early days this might have been the Market Research Mgr), who would take responsibility for data and analytics. The work might be outsourced to a specialist data/research team or combined with some in-house expertise.

In addition, the whole concept of the "Brand" began to take root. Brand Mgrs. began to proliferate as companies looked at the pioneer of effective Brand marketing, Procter & Gamble, and wanted to adopt and copy their, it seemed, proven success model. Brand Mgrs. were charged with being the "guardians of the brand". While no-one was quite sure what that meant! it seemed mostly about measuring and monitoring Brand awareness, propensity to purchase and brand sentiment. It also meant being the champion of the brand internally across the company. That usually also meant being the coordinator of brand planning, brand budgets, brand promotions, brand development and brand advertising. And in some instances having those skills reporting directly into them rather than being separated out.

But this era did particularly herald a step-change in the profile and power of Marketing. Marketing Directors began to appear on the main board. The Brand Mgr started to become a powerful figure of influence and responsibility. The team became more than just administrators of a promotions budget. They became responsible formally with Sales for top line revenue growth, and often

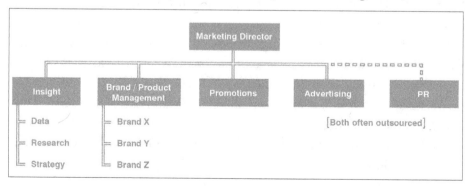

took on the Brand/Product P&L. They also had a much more involved role in the long term. No longer just about short term tactical campaigns and quarterly sales programmes. There was now also a key responsibility to use the data and insight to generate product development programmes which would keep the Brand alive and contemporary and compelling.

4. Now!

Today's world has seen a step change in complexity. We now live in this multi-channel, technology-enabled world of innovation, new ideas and constant change. Channels to market have proliferated and fragmented. It's no longer a simple world of TV, Print, Radio. Now add of course so much more whether via desktop, mobile, tablet, webcast, YouTube, Pinterest, Facebook, X/Twitter, social media monitoring generally, in-game advertising, pre-roll, SEO, SEM, blogs, eCRM, e-Commerce…the list goes on.

And yet, this has all fallen to the Marketing Department. No other team has stood up and tried to take this all on board. And typically no other team in the company would naturally have the skills or market understanding to adopt and embrace all this change and opportunity. So everyone now looks to Marketing. Tell us about these changing market /multi-channel /omni-channel conditions, how do we now reach out to our target audience (they are no longer where they used to be!), get us the data and insight that enables us to understand what marketing communications will work and what will not, conduct the tests that show how to engage with our target customers in this digital world, identify the new programmes and activities and product development which will ensure we remain /become successful!

No small challenge.

And so the Marketing department has had to evolve rapidly. It has had to take on and recruit new skills/ new people. It has had to expand simply to cover the basics. It now is expected to have skills in all these "new" areas and to understand mobile, social, Twitter etc etc. Over the course of the past decade marketing teams have grown in numbers (though not necessarily in comms spending budgets) and have become even more "centre stage". They are now the champions of not just the Brand, but also of the Customer. They now formulate the total customer engagement strategy. Instead of Sales driving Marketing (as used to happen), it's now the other way round. Marketing are the key. They are the ones who are at the heart of the business. It is their knowledge about digital and the changing market environment that is dictating the whole organisation's future strategy. It is now Marketing's relationship with IT that is the core team dynamic. It is how those two departments operate and collaborate and work effectively together that will ultimately decide who will be the future winners.

So in the next two diagrams /org structures, the first illustration shows how the Marketing skills set has proliferated and the range of new skills and functions the team had to adopt. The second chart next page shows how the better Marketing departments have come to terms with this, how they have reorganised to manage that proliferation to find a new simpler more streamlined more manageable and more effective org.solution.

As mentioned at the beginning of this note, there are no "right answers". And this has simply tried to show how things have changed, and by just how much! And what some possible ways of navigating the organisation through this changing dynamic period might look like.

(i)   Extended Marketing value chain /org.:

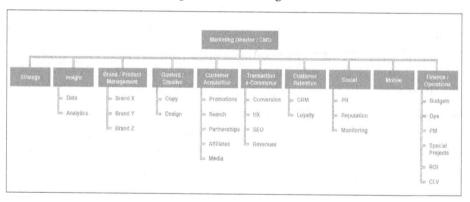

(ii)   A Streamlined /consolidated /multi-channel Marketing organisation structure:

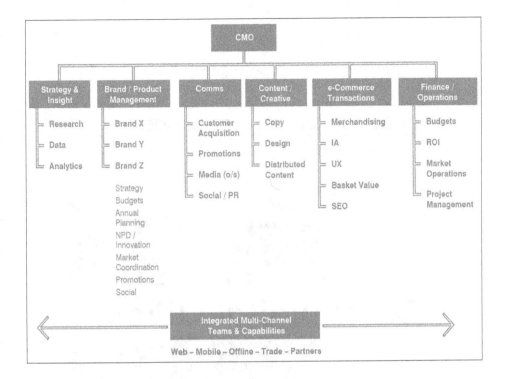

Chapter 18

A market perspective on digital leadership roles

Most every company of any size has these days appointed a Digital Leader. A recent Forbes survey showed that 88% of the Fortune 500 had a Chief Digital Officer as a key figure to lead their digital transformation journey.

Of course not all had the grand title of "Chief" and in some places they were more at the Head of level in the organisation but they still had the role as the "go-to" expert or champion in this space. Some had teams of hundreds reporting into them. Some in effect ran a more modest "centre of excellence" with the aim of setting the company-wide strategy and then acting in support of individual business units. It's been the B2C, consumer-facing business sectors especially in Retail who have led the way, pioneering and being among the first to explore and take advantage of new tech tools and new opportunities to strengthen consumer and customer engagement.

Who are the best CDOs, what sort of background would add most value to our organisation, what skills and organisation nous is required to make such an appointment a success?

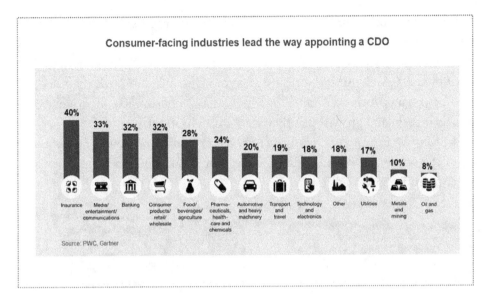

Consumer-facing industries lead the way appointing a CDO

Insurance	Media/ entertainment/ communications	Banking	Consumer products/ retail/ wholesale	Food/ beverages/ agriculture	Pharma- ceuticals, health- care and chemicals	Automotive and heavy machinery	Transport and travel	Technology and electronics	Other	Utilities	Metals and mining	Oil and gas
40%	33%	32%	32%	28%	24%	20%	19%	18%	18%	17%	10%	8%

Source: PWC, Gartner

The research is showing that most Chief Digital Officers or CDOs come from either a Marketing or Technology background. About a third are technologists who have grown up in IT and likely have a Computer Sciences or equivalent degree. Companies are choosing people with such background where they see core advantage coming from improvement in their IT platform as an enabler of change. It may be that they are not satisfied with their existing CTO or perhaps just frustrated at the complexity and blocks in their current legacy IT systems. So bring in a CDO who is also a Technical leader who can challenge and explore new IT solutions that might help the organisation leapfrog over its current stack. Possible but can be politically complex if the CDO and CTO are in conflict over strategy, budgets and direction.

More commonly we see CDOs coming from a Marketing /Commercial background. They may have been Marketers who gradually assumed control of all digital marketing to become more expert at the whole multi-channel consumer engagement. They may also have taken control of online sales and e-commerce and have developed a very broad area of expertise.

They are often in effect "Digital CEOs" with broad Brand, sales and marketing while also managing a growing and often significant online P&L.

No wonder that those CDOs who have the experience and stature to step-up to this mini CEO challenge are highly sought after. There are any number of rising stars, grown-up digital, who absolutely get the whole multi-channel opportunity. But companies making this sort of appointment also are looking for people with that C-level experience or quality, the stakeholder manager skills and political nous. Even for CDOs with the right skills mix, it is still not common for them to be formally at the senior ExCo /leadership /main Board level. They may find they do not report to the CEO but perhaps to the CFO or the CMO. And as a result their remit is more limited, their ability to effect change more curtailed and potentially constrained in driving the transformation and growth that they were brought in for.

In fact, we can see that companies have very different views of what they see in the scope and remit of their newly appointed CDO and what they are targeting and hope to achieve.

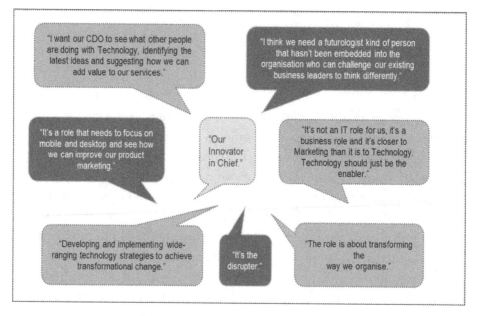

Given this variety of reasons for choosing a CDO, it is not surprising to find there are a number of different "typical" CDO remits:

Different types of CDO

All this CDO challenge and opportunity can perhaps best be captured and summarised in this interview here with Francois Gonczi when Global Digital Leader at EDF Energy:

"In appointing me, the company had several goals:

(i)   *To get closer to customers through digital experiences and data analysis*
(ii)   *To rethink and restructure internal operations and*
(iii)   *To devise disruptive new business models that would generate value.*

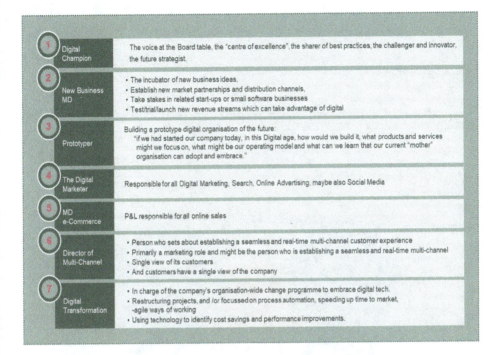

1	Digital Champion	The voice at the Board table, the "centre of excellence", the sharer of best practices, the challenger and innovator, the future strategist.
2	New Business MD	• The incubator of new business ideas, • Establish new market partnerships and distribution channels, • Take stakes in related start-ups or small software businesses • Test/trial/launch new revenue streams which can take advantage of digital
3	Prototyper	Building a prototype digital organisation of the future: "if we had started our company today, in this Digital age, how would we build it, what products and services might we focus on, what might be our operating model and what can we learn that our current "mother" organisation can adopt and embrace."
4	The Digital Marketer	Responsible for all Digital Marketing, Search, Online Advertising, maybe also Social Media
5	MD e-Commerce	P&L responsible for all online sales
6	Director of Multi-Channel	• Person who sets about establishing a seamless and real-time multi-channel customer experience • Primarily a marketing role and might be the person who is establishing a seamless and real-time multi-channel • Single view of its customers • And customers have a single view of the company
7	Digital Transformation	• In charge of the company's organisation-wide change programme to embrace digital tech. • Restructuring projects, and /or focussed on process automation, speeding up time to market, -agile ways of working • Using technology to identify cost savings and performance improvements.

These goals represented a major challenge for a traditional company like ours in a risk-adverse industry. Every small digitalisation project has required everyone around the table to be aligned and agreed. As CDO my role is to serve as the overarching organiser and orchestrator and go-to expert of our digital activities and to ensure a balance of empowering teams, providing oversight, reporting progress and ensuring that things stay on track."

Chapter 19

Digital eco-systems and incubators

With the rapid pace of technology change, many are looking to build eco-systems to help them compete, to access resources, to share investment funding, to provide more customer leverage, to share risk as well as a targeted upside reward.

Gartner defines it in this way: "a digital eco-system is an interdependent group of enterprises, people and/or things that share standardised digital technology platforms for a mutually beneficial purpose, such as commercial gain, innovation or common interest. Digital ecosystems enable you to interact with customers, partners, adjacent industries – and even your competition"

Most of the companies with the world's highest market capitalizations are Tech companies that generate much of their revenue from the digital eco-systems they have created. Many of these eco-systems are B2C plays. Others, such as Jabil's, represent B2B spaces. Some companies tackle both: Amazon, for example, ties together e-commerce, cloud computing, logistics and consumer electronics, while China's Tencent eco-system enables the company to provide a wide range of services including social media, gaming, finance, and cloud computing.

Here's a case study example from Siemens.

Siemens

They are a global Tech leader, a strong focus on innovation and collaboration and are ranked among the most successful digital tech leaders in the world. Key to this success according to a Boston Consulting survey was the establishment of the Siemens Research and Innovation Eco-system programme.

The aim was to design an eco-system that would enable Siemens to leverage its internal and external resources, capabilities, and networks, and to co-create innovative solutions that would meet the current and future needs of customers and stakeholders. The eco-system also needed to be scalable, adaptable, and resilient, to cope with the dynamic and uncertain market conditions.

Siemens set up a collaboration network with universities, research institutes, startups, and incubators, encouraging their participation by providing eg access to their own technology, funding, support, networking, mentorship, visibility, and recognition. Also there were a series of events, seminars and high profile public statements promoting this eco-system and giving praise and publicity to eg a new start-up partner which it otherwise might not have garnered.

Examples of the kind of initiatives this Siemens eco-system has fostered:

Deutsche Bahn: The Siemens programme co-created a digital solution for predictive maintenance of rail infrastructure, such as tracks, switches, and signals, using artificial intelligence and cloud computing.

Volkswagen: a digital co-solution for optimising the production of electric vehicles, using the internet of things and edge computing.

Airbus: a digital co-solution for additive manufacturing of aerospace components, using cloud computing and digital twin Ai.

In addition, through collaboration with partners, Siemens was able to bring a number of new initiatives and ventures to market:

MindSphere, an open cloud-based operating system for the industrial internet of things, offering customers a platform for data analytics and optimization.

Healthineers, a spin-off of its healthcare business, focuses on delivering innovative medical solutions.

Siemens Mobility emerged as a provider of comprehensive mobility solutions for rail and road transport.

Also having partnered with certain companies, Siemens found the collaboration so powerful that it led to a number of acquisitions such as Mendix, a leader in low-code application development platforms, Electrocon/PSS Cape, a provider of software solutions for power system protection and control and COMSA/Mentor, a specialist in electrical systems design.

The CEO of Siemens, Roland Busch, has commented: "our eco-system innovation programme has been a key engine for our growth and development for us, investment has paid back and we would certainly have missed out on new business opportunities without this partnership network."

To build an eco-system a company does not have to have the size and scale of a Siemens. Now, with the advent of digitalisation, data, analytics, new tech tools, new ways of engagement, so most every company has the platform and opportunity to seek out partnerships, sponsorships, co-customer investment, joint ventures, allying with start-ups, supporting new ventures and all to help to widen their market reach and remit and accelerate their efforts to bring new products /services to market and reach new geographies and new customers.

The 5 key lessons from successful digital eco-system innovators can be summarised in this way:

1. *Innovation ecosystems do require dedicated resource to set them up.* It needs an investment in people. The funds may well come from the partners. But what characterises the successes here is that commitment to making key dedicated people available.

2. *Finding partners with the same culture and chemistry.* Like any partnership it has its up and downs and what works best is where the people leaders of each team get on, share the same values

and ideals, and have the right chemistry to solve work problems collaboratively.

3. *Shared goals*: important too to find partners who truly have the same priorities eg a determination to develop the leading product in a specific sector, and eg a readiness to accept that breakeven and profit may be several years out.

4. *Ecosystems need to be scalable, adaptable, and resilient* to cope with the changing and uncertain market conditions and customer needs.

5. *Creating a supportive culture* of innovation and entrepreneurship encourages experimentation and readiness to learn from failure as well from success.

Here's another example from Huawei, the Chinese Networking/Telco and their commitment to investing and building out their eco-system as another means to secure competitive advantage.

Huawei

With a view to building a digital ecosystem in the Southeast Asia region, Huawei has made an $81 million investment with the theme "Innovate for a Digital Asia-Pacific." Over the next three years, Huawei will invest in setting up open labs, enabling cloud developers, and cultivating ICT talent in the Southeast Asian countries. Huawei's Region President James Wu has unveiled its "developer enablement plan, saying that it's aimed at supporting digital economy growth and cultivating an ecosystem in the region.

We want to empower developers and promote young talent in Southeast Asia. We have over 30 years of experience and capabilities in the ICT sector. Through APIs and development platforms, we will open up our capabilities to our partners in the region…this is a huge opportunity for developers to create targeted solutions to the digitalization of industries and grow their own business. By working together, we can dream bigger and fly higher."

And some further examples:

Danske Bank
Established a network of partners to create an online Utilities portal

- Aggregator of real time data feeds from realtors, utility and service providers
- Type in post code number of bedrooms in the house or square metres
- Get an estimate of running costs, local taxes, utilities etc.-provide better financing advice, customer support and service
- Become the first stop on a house search

Home Depot
- Launched the Wink Hub connected home network
- "Wink is the quick and simple way to connect you and your home. Manage hundreds of smart products from the best brands in one simple app"
- "Wink allows smart products from different brands (e.g. providing lighting, heating, phone, computing, TV services) to speak the same wireless language so you can easily control them via the Wink app".
- Home Depot has established partnerships with many of its suppliers to create this connected home ecosystem

Philips Healthcare
- Team up with Salesforce.com to build a future health care platform
- An ecosystem of developers building healthcare applications
- Enable collaboration and unified workflow between doctors and patients
- Partnerships with self-care providers, prevention regimes, diagnostics and treatment
- All revolving and tied into a Philips eco-world

Fiat
Partnering with TomTom, Facebook, Reuters, TuneIn and others to create a Uconnect platform

- To provide drivers with real time news, communication, entertainment, navigation

- Looking in the future to be a one-stop portal for all driver needs from insurance to car servicing

Eco-systems are being seen as a powerful new means to drive business growth and development. It's been described as a "re-imagining of industry and sector boundaries.
– Gartner report

The ongoing digital revolution is reshaping customer expectations…digital pioneers are extending the value proposition…asking what new customer opportunities exist across traditional boundaries…can we leverage partnerships and connections to find new revenues?

Greater digital collaboration between G20 companies and entrepreneurs could result in an additional $1.5 trillion in global GDP, an uplift of 2.2 percent, with the top 20 percent of companies committed to collaboration achieving higher levels of revenue growth.
– McKinsey

Technology is the key and driving solo is no longer an option.
– Jeff Bezos

Companies that draw 50 percent or more of their revenue from digital ecosystems saw growth and profits 27 to 32 percent higher than average.
– MIT Sloan Management

Twenty years ago we were building small software systems that may have done one thing and operated in isolation. Now you have platform as a service, infrastructure as a service, security as a service, and all of these systems are starting to integrate.
– Wired magazine review

87% of large companies say that open and shared innovation networks will be critical to achieve higher levels of future business performance.
– Accenture survey

In terms of building a successful eco-system, further research from Accenture has helped identify the six key components that need to be in place:

1. **API-enabled**: application programming interfaces as the enablers of faster, easier, seamless collaboration and integration
2. **Analytics**: have a core *joint and collaborative* AI /Advanced Analytics capability to identify new sources of opportunity
3. **Real-time**: build the networking capability that can operate with real-time data /insight feeds
4. **Interoperability**: use shared and common /open source data standards and communication protocols
5. **Innovation culture**: empower and enable an entrepreneurial culture to game-change and capture new business opportunities
6. **Share the passion**: from the CEO and ExCo through the rest of the eco-system team and partner groups

★ ★ ★

As companies examine and explore these new alliance and open-system opportunities, so at the same time they are often developing them as new businesses. This is frequently on a stand-alone basis, with their own P&L and management teams. And to encourage more entrepreneurial freedom and empowerment, they are also reaching out to Private Equity to co-fund or alternatively establishing their own incubator style start-up /new venture environments where they might launch several eco-system type initiatives, take stakes rather than acquire, share the risk with entrepreneurs who want to retain some ownership and encourage a whole wave of new initiative-taking.

It can be an exciting area of business development and useful to consider just how much support, investment and activity is going on. Looking at just the key UK-based Digital and Tech business incubators, the London digital tech new venture scene has experienced a rapid rise in incubator and accelerator programmes in the past few years, much faster than any other European city.

Across the UK, research has identified 205 incubators and 163 accelerators supporting an estimated 3,450 businesses, plus 3,660 new businesses a year. These provide up to c.£150m annually in startup investment, according to *Wired* and the *Business Incubators and Accelerators*. By way of example, the top 5 London incubator groups are:

1. Seedcamp
Backed by major venture capitalists, angel investors, and corporate entities, Seedcamp has provided early-stage and micro-seed funding to more than 650

entrepreneurs from over 150 startups within 28 industries. Seedcamp-backed companies have raised over $900m in follow-on funding on a $1bn valuation.

2. Startupbootcamp

A global accelerator with 21 programmes in major cities including London, New York, Amsterdam, and many more. Each location focuses on a specific tech vertical such as commerce, finance, food, energy, and transportation.

London's Startupbootcamp offers three-month accelerated development programming to early-stage FinTech startups.

3. RockStart

RockStart supports scale-ups with industry focused expertise. The aim is to provide ongoing strategic development through highly qualified corporate collaborators and partnership opportunities.

4. Techstars

"A global force in Tech" with accelerator programs in software, health, retail, mobility, and more, Techstars has supported 1,024 total companies, raising a combined total of over $3.8bn on a $9.9bn market cap.

Global network of mentors and corporate partners, 3 months of office space, and "perks" worth over $1m.

5. Founders Factory

Founders Factory provides both early and late-stage programming for entrepreneurs. With access to a global network of entrepreneurs and top-tier digital talent, Founders Factory has invested in over 200 businesses across six key technology sectors including media, education, beauty, travel, artificial intelligence, and finance. With backing from Aviva, Guardian Media Group, L'Oréal, and others.

Other incubator groups include:

- Imperial College London Enterprise Lab
- Innovify Ventures
- Entrepreneurs Trust
- Runway
- Capital Innovators

In addition, a growing number of major corporates now have their own very successful e-Ventures investment programmes building out stakes in a number of related companies. The idea is to learn from these new start-ups, be able to potentially take on their ideas and Tech, and ultimately produce new and innovative products and revenue streams.

Companies such as Unilever, Zurich Insurance Group, Microsoft, Intel, Barclays, News Corp UK, JLAB (John Lewis), Tesco, Virgin and many others are doing this,

One of the best and most successful is Telefonica's **WAYRA:**

- "We have set up the Telefonica digital technology eco-system
- As part of a global innovation network open to partners, Wayra commits to the internationalisation and scalability of start-ups.
- investment start-up hubs in 10 countries across Europe and Latin America
- Over 10 years, we have invested in some 800 companies across a range of sectors.
- in the UK, our incubator is housed on the 4th floor of the Telefonica central London head office. Telefonica execs are encouraged to drop-in to see what's going on!
- These Wayra supported startups are working to provide disruptive solutions to Telefónica and its customers."

Chapter 20

Industry 4.0

Leading B2B companies are using Digital Tech to power sales and profit growth

Over the past few years McKinsey has been measuring and evaluating the impact and potential that Digital Tech can have for B2B companies. The message: B2B companies need to wake up to the opportunities Digital Technology can bring, with those who are investing in this area significantly outperforming peers and rivals who are not.

Part of the McKinsey survey has been to assess how ready a company is for Digital Transformation and how developed are its skills and systems to take advantage. There are a number of successful B2B companies who have developed strong Digital capabilities. Organisations like Cisco, Boeing, Wolverine, Ford, Caterpillar, Texas Instruments and others. But most lag the B2C average and closing that gap is going to be crucial. Top-quartile Digital performers grow more sales, earn more profits, and deliver more value to shareholders than the rest of the B2B field.

Top Digital B2B players outperform their peers

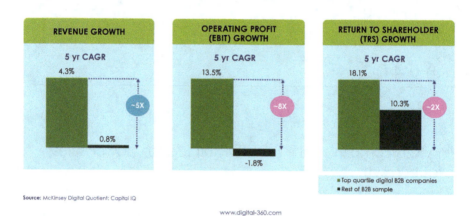

Source: McKinsey Digital Quotient; Capital IQ

www.digital-360.com

B2B companies trail their B2C counterparts in digitization.

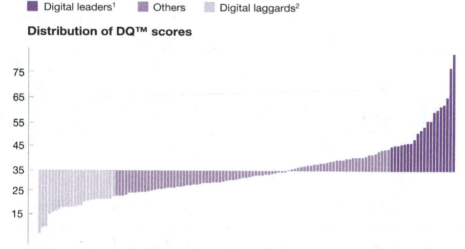

DQ™ score is calculated on a scale of 0 to 100 as the average score of the 4 equally weighted dimensions: Culture, Strategy, Capabilities and Organization.

[1]Digital leaders are defined as companies with a DQ score equal to or above 50.
[2]Digital laggards are defined as companies with a DQ score below 25.

McKinsey&Company |

Some of this is not a complete surprise, of course, since the digital ecosystem can be tougher to establish and navigate for B2B companies. Their sales forces face, for example, a far more complex purchasing environment, with multiyear deal cycles in some cases, lengthy RFP processes, and the involvement of many vendors, decision makers, and influencers.

While these complexities are significant, it would be a mistake to use them as an excuse for falling short in some key areas. Digitisation has made consistent, high-quality customer interactions a competitive differentiator. Right now, however, selling models remain largely hitched to offline channels. It's hard for business buyers to get the pertinent and personalised information they need and want from supplier websites and social platforms and harder still to buy directly (though often that is a supplier's intentional strategy).

In addition, while B2B sales teams are working harder to close deals that often involve multiple rounds and many more decision makers, they often lack the real-time analytics and digital tools they need to manage the sale profitably by knowing whom to court with what offer or when to conduct personal outreach.

Incremental changes or pilot efforts can provide benefits, but they aren't likely to significantly close the gap.

Leading B2B companies however do embrace an "all in" digital tech strategy, knowing it's crucial for making needed core changes. And they don't focus on just digitising sales and customer interactions, but on harnessing digital assets internally to enable their teams to perform better. "Industry 4.0" has become a byword for a full-on review of how digital tools and solutions can unlock significant performance gains across the whole supply chain through automation, real-time connectivity and data and predictive maintenance.

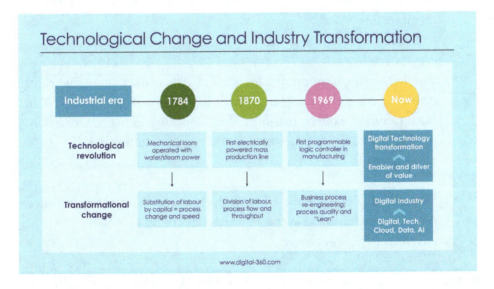

PWC found that Industrial leaders are planning to commit up to $1trillion to Industry 4.0 –around 5% of revenue p.a. A major focus of these investments will be on digital technologies like sensors or connectivity devices, and on software and applications like manufacturing execution systems.

Companies like Ford, Caterpillar, Wolverine, Cisco, Siemens, Bayer, Samsung and others are committing to digital transformation because customers are demanding it, competitive pressures are forcing it and they realise that driving through these changes can uncover new sources of profit and revenue growth. They are also very aware of these sort of market findings:

- 81% of Purchasing/ Procurement Managers said they would choose a supplier that offers a fast, easy-to-use online ordering option over an equal supplier who does not. The reasons were: (i) do business at our convenience, (ii) save time, and (iii) easily monitor order status
  – *Hybris*

- B2B e-Commerce in the US alone is set to reach $2 trillion in 2025 including through business networks and EDI as well as suppliers' e-commerce sites. This is twice that of the B2C market
  – *Forrester report*

- 65% of B2B companies in a recent Oracle survey said they now sold direct using e-commerce and 80% of companies in that survey said that they are now actively reviewing this opportunity, whether to launch or invest further
  – *Oracle*

- The IoT segment accounted for around 20% market share due to its pivotal role in connecting and enhancing industrial processes. IoT in manufacturing collect real-time data, enabling enhanced decision-making, predictive maintenance, and resource optimization.
  – *Forrester report*

- 57% of total sales are predicted through e-commerce by B2B companies. A number are claiming average growth rates of up to 30% +
  – *Forrester /JP Morgan report*

Industry 4.0 is made possible by a host of cutting-edge technologies, including:

- Internet of Things (IoT): IoT refers to a network of interconnected devices and sensors embedded with software and network connectivity which enable them to collect and exchange data. IoT is the main foundation forming Industry 4.0's interconnectivity.

- AI smart software that is able to automatically process data, learn, reason, generate insights, and act autonomously. AI can facilitate automation for efficiency and predictive analytics to enhance decision-making.
- Big data analytics: collection and analysis of large amounts of data to enable informed decision-making. Turning seemingly random raw information into actionable insights by identifying patterns and trends.
- Automation: Industry 4.0's smart factories won't be complete without automation— the use of robots and automated machines to perform tasks with minimal to no human intervention.
- Additive manufacturing (3D printing): manufacturing (printing) three-dimensional objects from digital models, layer by layer 3D printing is a major game-changer in Industry 4.0, enabling rapid prototyping and customization.
- Augmented Reality (AR): AR overlays digital information into real-world objects and environments. It can act as a bridge between the digital and physical worlds, aiding personnel in maintenance, troubleshooting, and training.

The main area of Industry 4.0 impact is in the Supply Chain, and companies are finding that data and data analytics can be a rich source of innovation. They are especially finding that if they establish an effective eco-system with

Data Analytics across the Supply Chain

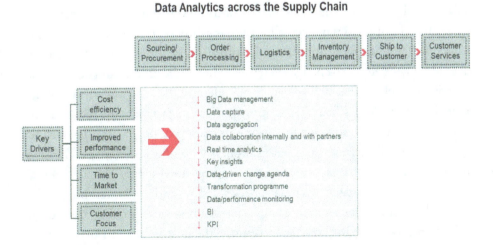

suppliers and partners and with customers, that they can now take an integrated and complete end-to-end view of parts, process, inventory and distribution, drive hard to a truly just-in-time solution that can provide a win-win-win for all parties and a major reason for partners and suppliers, and also customers, to sign-up, participate and integrate.

Data and data analytics have a key part to play in identifying opportunities and Machine Learning will ramp up innovation opportunities and ideas and raise the bar on what is possible.

Ford, for example, has used its plant in Cologne, Germany as a key hub for eco-system and "industry 4.0" innovation and change. The plant manufactures 6 types of engine transmission and also supplies Mazda and Volvo across Europe. Total volumes are more than 1 million transmissions each year and there are a significant number of custom variations. The production process involves many different parts from multiple suppliers located in different countries. All this had created an environment where inventory was high and there were frequent delays due to non-availability of parts and the production process was slower than target.

Ford has now introduced its "Material Flows Wireless Parts". This is a wireless messaging infrastructure of 220 RFID (radio frequency identification) tags installed as "Where Call" buttons. Each tag is associated with a specific parts number. A core wifi network has been set up throughout the plant, mobile PCs are mounted at key stages on the production and assembly lines and also at staging points in the warehouse and on the fork lift trucks. Press the "where call" button and the "parts needed" message is immediately directed to the key warehouse area for that part. The supplier is also automatically notified so they can keep track of inventory. They are now responsible for just in time availability and accountable for any failure. As a result of this the assembly line worker stays on station and is trained when to call for replenishment to maintain continuous production. "It's intelligent automation". Ford are now developing AI techniques that could potentially step-change even this "where call" process and develop the predictive modelling that will automatically identify the replenishment timing. So far this initiative has had a 20% improvement in productivity, reduced on-hand inventory to 24 hours, led to a near elimination of down-time and helped forge more effective partnerships with suppliers who now have the visibility and can take more initiative their end as well to improve total supply chain efficiency.

While many manufacturers today are developing and implementing similar real-time inventory management initiatives, others are also looking beyond the production process and at how best to engage the customer to ensure growing demand. One leading example is Cisco. They have been at the forefront in adopting lessons from the B2C environment and enabling their customers to buy anytime anywhere anyhow, a true multi-channel capability.

Cisco are now seen as a leading edge B2B case study in this regard and their journey down this path was kick-started some years ago. This extract below from an interview with Blake Salle, the then Cisco SVP Sales:

> *We were doing our annual review and we had one customer who had never purchased from Cisco before and who placed an order online for nearly $100m. The immediate reaction was "hey, where did that come from!" and then our second reaction was:*
>
>> *Let's get the Sales team down there straight away". But you know what, when we got in touch, they said ok, no need for your Sales people to visit, just make it easy for us to buy from you.*
>
> *What we didn't realise in the early days is also just how important it was to appeal to all online customers big and small. Then we saw buyers from small customers naturally joining the larger companies and buyers still at smaller companies suddenly and dramatically increasing their online order size. And of course it's a small world and word of mouth is strong. So if we'd not dealt with them properly when they were small they sure as anything weren't going to deal with us when they got big.*

Cisco: how to buy…it's a main navigation tool on their website:

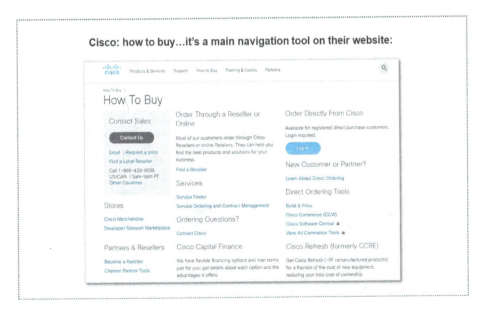

Blake Salle was at the forefront in pushing Cisco into multi-channel selling and still today the Cisco web site is the most B2B sales /buyer friendly and helpful. The main online navigation has *at the top level* a key tab: "How to Buy" and every option is then laid out: call us, click here for our distribution centres and stores, buy through our partners, here's a list of our resellers and order directly from them, or buy directly online from us, and by the way here's the Cisco App for product specific info and phone numbers for local support near you.

This is a customer /buyer capability which seems so right to set-up and establish but still so many B2B organisations are slow to embrace and implement these sort of initiatives, still relying on the traditional Sales visit to take orders, part implementing new production techniques, still slow to develop open systems and real-time automation in the supply chain, still hesitating about new technology opportunities. It is of course a significant investment to do these things but critical if at all feasible to have the vision and plan and find ways bit by bit to get there, especially if, as Cisco and others are finding, it can open up new sources and ways to drive revenue growth, improve efficiency and cost of delivery and so provide an attractive return and gain.

Chapter 21

Digital IQ

Organisation readiness to drive transformation and change

McKinsey and PWC have been pioneering the idea of a Digital IQ index, measuring a company's awareness and knowledge around Digital Technology change and most critically an organisation's readiness to embrace and implement digital and data transformation.

This index has been developed to help companies determine how ambitious should their change programmes be, how likely it is that they might succeed, what might be the most realistic timetable to set and expect for delivery and what training and support needs might be required to help the organisation and its workforce achieve the kind of changes that are being targeted.

So this index is a crucial audit, an excellent and necessary reality-check. It can be conducted internally by eg the HR team or an outside independent consultancy who can report perhaps most objectively on the possible challenges and blocks that need to be managed and overcome. Transformation is an easy word to say but of course can be very difficult to implement with great success and as we read elsewhere in this book, sadly most transformation programmes do fail. So it can be vital to have this kind of "IQ" check right at the start to potentially provide a blueprint for moving forwards.

McKinsey have carried out a series of Digital IQ surveys and client checks globally especially over the past few years. They are able to show the state of an organisation's ability to cope with large scale change and how that ability compares with eg others in the sector and with the wider business community. If an organisation is shown to be one of the "laggards" then it can be the necessary wake-up call that will indicate the amount of preparation and support required if any major change programme is to be successfully implemented.

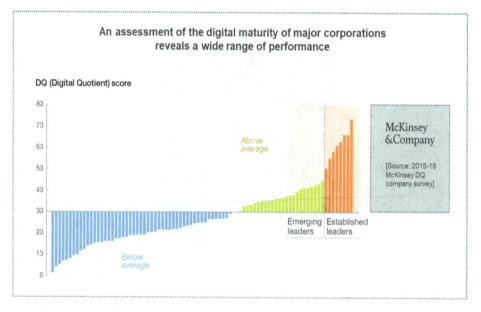

The criteria that are employed in this audit are relatively simple and straightforward but the evidence collected and the benchmarking against others can be very revealing.

Digital IQ

Key tests:

1. *Vison and commitment clearly set-out*
2. *Alignment around the Executive team (that this is a priority)*
3. *Readiness to invest*
4. *Financial stability to carry the costs of transformation*
5. *Right skills and talent*
6. *Resources available*

7. *Culture /people ready*
8. *Analytics in place to measure /monitor*
9. *Data platforms in good state*
10. *Agile methodologies established*

At the most basic level, the IQ audit can evaluate these criteria, and in the context of what are the best practices and benchmarks, then score and rate an individual company. These scores can be a simple score out of 10 with a max IQ of 100. Any score less that 50 would indicate the organisation is not ready yet for any large-scale transformation and that significant preparatory work is required to enable the company to deliver. A score between 50 and 65 suggests proceed, but with caution, map out the roadmap carefully, pick some of the easiest projects to start with and meantime, work to start filling in the IQ gaps. A score north of 70 would be regarded as positive and an encouraging sign to move ahead, while still being mindful of where there might be needs in the organisation for additional help and support.

This IQ audit is just a guide. It's not intended to be by itself the go /no-go decision-maker. Some companies may be in distress and have little choice about delay and need to get on as best they can. Others will start but perhaps set a longer time-frame to allow the organisation to get up-to-speed and get more confident and comfortable with a transformation agenda. Those who score well will have the knowledge that they can move ahead, set more challenging goals and timetables, still keep an eye on the needs for support and help, but be able to envisage continuing success if they deliver their transformation goals.

Chapter 22

Does investment in digital pay back?

An introduction to the new "Digital Masters"

Does investment in Digital Technology pay-back? Is it a long term play building a platform for the future that may perhaps deliver 5 years out? Or can investment *now* deliver early wins and results?

There's significant pressure on companies these days to "get digital". This can range from hiring in a new "Chief Digital Officer" to re-launching e-Commerce, expanding social media, setting up advanced Analytics and data mining, automating for self-serve, generating new business leads online, even taking stakes in myriad start-ups…the list of potential opportunities is endless but what's it all worth?

For the first time there's now some reassurance that it *is* all worthwhile. It's not just about doing it because competitors are, or the brokers and analysts expect you to, or because the Marketing and Sales teams are saying you have to, there is now some strong proof and validation that it does truly result in increased profitability to the point of leading sector ROI.

This proof comes from the first truly rigorous piece of research. It was carried out by MIT. Published recently in the Harvard Business Review and also a book called Leading Digital. The top line shows that those who become "Digital Masters" are *26% more profitable* than their industry peers. Those who lag behind in this digital race are 24% less profitable.

It's an extraordinary finding and the research covers some 300 + companies across the world and across different industry sectors. Time and again the MIT team found these high levels of success repeated. So what's going on, what lies behind the research, what's it take to become a "Digital Master"?

To begin with the Research team found there were basically 4 types of companies. These could be categorised as Beginners, "Fashionistas", Conservatives and Digital Masters. And this categorisation was at its most stark when the comparison was done by different industry sector. So it was more likely to find Masters in Retail or Personal Banking. Whereas in B2B Manufacturing, most organisations were well behind the digital curve, despite evidence that even in that sector, those who did invest did get results.

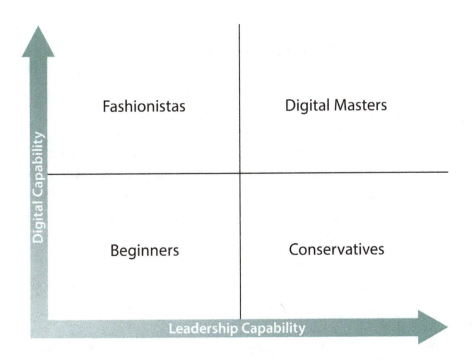

Four levels of digital mastery

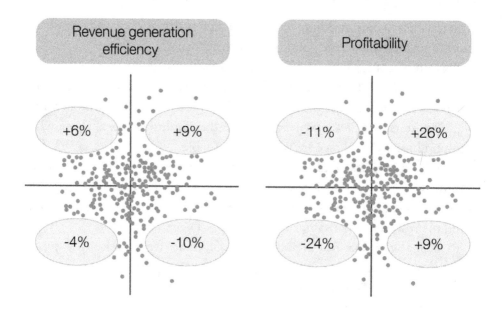

Basket of indicators:
- Revenue/employee
- Fixed-assets turnover

Basket of indicators:
- EBIT margin
- Net profit margin

Digital masters outperform

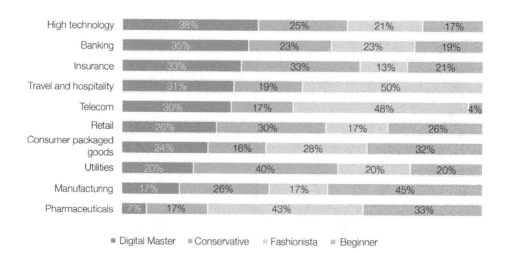

Digital mastery by industry

The MIT research has also highlighted what are the key success factors. While it was for sure about the appetite to invest and the relative amount of investment, it was *also* about the execution and delivery. Some companies were shown to have invested in teams and technology platforms but the investment was kept siloed, the digital team stood on its own, it functioned more as a separate division, there was little integration with the core business, and so little change in the basic business processes and operations. That led to resentment on all sides, frustration in the digital team who were limited in what they could achieve and resentment in the core business who felt much needed investment funds were being diverted.

What led to success was to marry the digital strategy and investment alongside building the digital transformation capability *inside* the core business. The research shows that it was essential to develop the change and implementation leadership skills, to ramp up the PMO team, to identify the core projects and staff them up with leadership and change delivery expertise, that what helped was having a core Steering Committee, led by the CEO, that held weekly or monthly reviews, in-depth, around the change agenda, milestones and progress, so that everyone saw this was a top CEO item and needed the attention and priority to make things happen.

Case Study

Asian Paints is one of these "Digital Masters". They are India's largest paint company and operate across Asia with revenues of c. $2.5bn. Former President and CIO there Manish Choksi attributes their success to "successive waves of digital tech transformation".

Their aim has been to globalise, maintain high levels of growth (they have hit 10% cagr over past 15 yrs), and to do that while increasing efficiency, innovating and enhancing the customer experience through digital engagement and also important for them, to continue to reduce their environmental impact. "We are spread over 120 locations and deal directly with some thirty thousand retailers so getting our growth strategy right around digital is critical for us".

Among other things they have established an industry awarded best-in-class e-Commerce platform which all the operating subsidiaries must use, they have one unified and now centralised customer ordering process which is self-serve and online and standardised, the Sales team have embraced this online order process and have changed their role from order-takers to strategic advisors to existing customers while adding a key new business/new customer focus to their work and revenue targets. In addition, steps in the supply chain have been automated with new technology tools and workflow software wherever possible to reduce the level of manpower and error, and they have also taken advantage of new Cloud-based partner software to better manage relationships. There is now a more in-depth data and performance management capability and that has led to more insight around product profitability and led to the roll-out of a new premium product range to meet a new identified customer segment need.

All-in-all a significant set of steps and as Manish Choksi acknowledges (former President of Asia Paints and now a non-exec Director there): "the road ahead still continues, our strategy is built on our ongoing digital technology investment, we expect our digital transformation will continue well into our future". Right now Asian Paints are rated as "the leading digital masters in their industry in South Asia"

To summarise: the MIT Research team distilled what they found as the 4 key practices which marked out companies like Asian Paints, Unilever, Procter & Gamble, Seven Eleven Japan, EMC, Codelco, American Express, Burberry and a host of others as "Digital Masters". Those 4 key steps are:

1. *"Framing the digital challenge"*: A unified consolidated CEO and Board decision that Digital is key to the company's future and the identification of the digital vision, targets and future state.

2. *"Focussing the investment"*: Putting in place the funding for the transformation

3. *"Mobilising the organisation"*: Communicating constantly, reinforcing the same set of messages and goals, using Social Media tools to encourage bottom-up ideation, sharing the rewards and upside as progress gets made.

4. *"Sustaining the transition"*: recognising this is not a one-off exercise, but the need to build a sustainable innovation and change culture, a

culture that rewards change and does not condemn well-intentioned failure, an ability to measure progress both internally and externally vs. competition and ensuring a continuous programme of employee awareness-building, education and technical literacy.

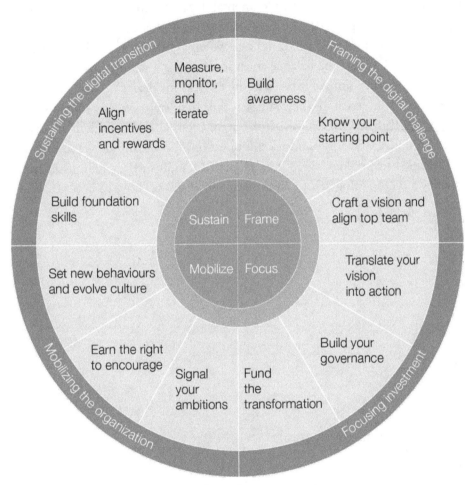

The digital transformation compass

★ ★ ★

Becoming a "Digital Master" or put another way, leading a successful digital transformation of the company, was rated the biggest challenge facing all organisations no matter what the industry sector in a recent McKinsey study.

It's being able to reach beyond the short term earnings and profits targets and seeing the future 5 year picture and market state, it's being able to see what needs to change, about setting priorities and perhaps most critically somehow finding the funding and investment to enable the change and transformation to take place. At some companies, there may be no choice, it may be a do or die move to survive. But often there is no crisis, as at Asian Paints, yet it requires the Board and CEO to make a fundamental decision about how to succeed in the long term, a reappraisal of strategy, a review of all budget spend, a refocus of effort and activity, a stop on things that weren't clearly about a digital future, a readiness to leverage the balance sheet if necessary, a willingness to consider radical alliances or joint ventures, a desire to "test trial learn".

In the MIT research they suggest this first step for any organisation considering this major change: carry out an internal and confidential survey across the entire workforce and ask this question: "how ready are we to succeed in the digital technology age?" The Digital IQ audit in the previous chapter provides a methodology from McKinsey and PWC on how to best go about that.

Chapter 23

"Courage to care"

A final thought /observation about the *"courage to care"*.

I was inspired by a lecture given by Joe Garner when CEO of Nationwide Building Society. Nationwide is a UK Bank with 15 million "members" or customers. They have been consistently voted as one of the best large companies to work for and have won numerous customer care and customer service awards.

When asked about how Nationwide achieves its high levels of employee commitment and engagement, Joe talked about building a culture and spirit which has "the courage to care"

I find it's an inspiring idea which often gets lost in the noise and with all the other demands, priorities and messages that companies have to manage.

Here however are 3 companies that also try to adopt and embrace this.

1. Beiersdorf

Core Values

"Our four Core Values have shaped our corporate culture since the very beginning and are still relevant today. They act as our guiding light and ensure that we speak one language across Beiersdorf. Moreover, they provide us with an orientation for our daily behaviour and serve as a benchmark, we can measure ourselves against."

- **Care** – We act responsibly towards our colleagues, consumers, brands, our society and our environment.
- **Simplicity** – We strive for clarity and consistency, make decisions quickly and pragmatically and focus on what's essential.
- **Courage** – We are committed to bold objectives, take initiative, learn from our mistakes and see change as an opportunity.
- **Trust** – We say what we mean, keep our promises and treat others with respect.

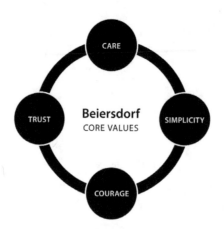

2. Merck

Merck Values - the Foundation of Our Success

Our company values are the yardstick for our thinking and actions. They are the essence of what ties us together today and tomorrow.

At Merck, we do business on the basis of common values. Our success is based on courage, achievement, responsibility, respect, integrity, and transparency. These values determine our actions in our daily dealing with customers and business partners as well as in our teamwork and our collaboration with each other.

**Courage Achievement Responsibility Respect Integrity
Transparency**

Courage opens the door to the future.
- Courage requires trust in one's own abilities.
- Courage leads to a healthy self-perception.
- Courage supports the competence needed to execute decisions in change processes.
- Courage means: We challenge ourselves.
- Courage opens us to new ideas

Responsibility determines our entrepreneurial actions.
- Responsibility characterizes our behaviour towards customers, employees, investors and service providers.
- Responsibility means treating our natural resources with care and vigilantly protecting our environment.
- Responsibility determines our business decisions, which we jointly endorse.
- Responsibility means setting a good example.
- Responsibility leads to recognition and acceptance of our business activities.

3. Holmen Iggesund

Core values
- The Group's strategic HR vision is that Holmen Iggesund shall be a company distinguished by employees who, with courage, commitment and responsibility, perform at their best. Also, we believe that when our people are involved in and proud of their company, they are engaged in their personal continued development and the success of everyone here.
- Holmen's shared values are courage, commitment and responsibility.

Courage
Courage to act. Holmen's employees are action oriented and make decisions that lead to tangible results. The company rewards innovative thinking that leads to improvements and solves challenges. The Group believes in transparency internally within the company and with the surrounding community.

Responsibility

Responsibility based on sensitivity and skills. Holmen's employees create participation by involving each other, sharing ideas and providing opportunities to exercise influence. Holmen takes action at an early stage and demonstrates drive when tackling challenges from the environment in which we operate and is proactive about improvement. Holmen's employees are professional in the way in which we run and develop our operations and we foster sustainable relationships with customers, stakeholders, colleagues and the surrounding community.

★ ★ ★

Jeffrey Pfeffer, the Harvard Professor, has written and lectured for a long time about building and encouraging the workforce to care and how companies can build "advantage through people".

His take is that:

> *Sustainable competitive advantage has proved elusive for companies. While making enormous investments in technology, research, and state-of-the-art marketing, many of today's managers continue to ignore the single most important factor in achieving and maintaining competitive success: people. Yet all evidence indicates that the source of competitive advantage, in this age of demanding digital technology and data transformation, may rest more and more on how a company manages and cares for its employees.*